NGLAND, AT KENNINGTON OVAL.

PHOTOGRAPH.

100 YEARS OF
TEST CRICKET
ENGLAND V AUSTRALIA

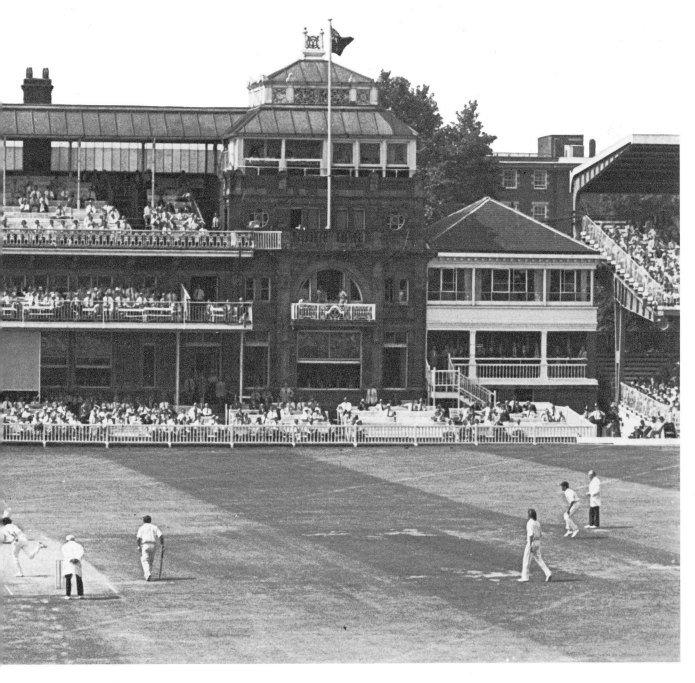

THE ASHES

...o goes back with the urn, the urn...
...teel. Read and Tylecote return, ...
...welkin will ring loud, ...
...eat crowd will feel proud, ...
...rlow and Bates with the urn, ...
...st coming home with the urn.

100 YEARS OF TEST CRICKET
ENGLAND V AUSTRALIA

David Foster and Peter Arnold

Foreword by Tony Greig

HAMLYN

LONDON · NEW YORK · SYDNEY · TORONTO

The pictures on the preliminary pages and
end-papers are as follows:
Front end-paper: England v Australia at
the Kennington Oval, 1882.
Back end-paper: Melbourne Ground in
1975.
Half-title: Lord's Cricket Ground, England
v Australia, 1975.
Facing title-page: The Ashes urn.

The front cover pictures are of Tony
Greig and Greg Chappell, with, inset,
W. G. Grace and S. E. Gregory.
The back cover picture is of David Lloyd
and Australians jubilant at his dismissal,
1974–75.

Published by
The Hamlyn Publishing Group Limited
London · New York · Sydney · Toronto
Astronaut House, Feltham, Middlesex, England

Copyright © 1977 The Hamlyn Publishing Group Limited

ISBN 0 600 36746 0

Photoset by Tradespools Ltd, Frome, Somerset
Printed in Hong Kong

Foreword

I was pleased when the authors asked me to write the foreword to this book, because England versus Australia is something special in cricket. Part of the reason for this lies in the great history of the matches between the countries.

The match which began at Melbourne a hundred years ago (on Thursday March 15, 1877) has come to be recognized as the first official Test. Charles Bannerman took the first ball and scored the first century, and in the succeeding hundred years great deeds have been performed, great controversies have raged and great matches taken place.

Players who play in the matches now or in the future are treading the same paths of such as W. G. Grace, Hobbs, Trumper and Bradman. Today has its heroes, too, and Lillee and Thomson will be legendary figures for perhaps the next hundred years.

All the players who have played in England–Australia matches are named in this book. Most of the greatest are pictured, and when one reads of their performances – Bradman's 300 in a day or Laker's 19 wickets – one is tempted to say 'follow that'.

That others will follow it, and try to better it, is certain. Drama and excitement is always on the cards when England play Australia, and the special magic which players and spectators feel every time a new battle for the Ashes starts will last as long as cricket. In my opinion, that will be a long time.

Tony Greig

1877 The First Test Match

Australia won the first Test match ever, which was played at Melbourne Cricket Ground from March 15 to 17, 1877. Australia's captain was Dave Gregory, England's James Lillywhite – both formidable men with huge beards.

Australia's batting hero was Charles Bannermann, who faced the first ball in Test cricket and was undefeated on 165 when he had to retire hurt with a split finger; the next highest score in the Australian first innings of 245 was 18, which shows how Bannermann dominated play. The other hero was the fast left arm bowler Kendall, who took 7 England wickets for 55 in their second innings of 108, to ensure victory by 45 runs. Thus started a great series of encounters – before a crowd that at one time reached twelve thousand.

England had excuses ready for their defeat: they had only arrived in Melbourne the day before the game after a stormy sea crossing from New Zealand: there they had left Ed Pooley, their only wicket-keeper, in police custody following a brawl.

Another Test was quickly arranged: this time England won by 4 wickets.

1
A print of Melbourne Cricket Ground dating from just before the first Test.

2
Australian Test cricketers in 1878.
Back row: J. Blackham, T. Horan, G. Bailey, J. Conway (manager), A. Bannerman, C. Bannerman, W. Murdoch.
Seated: F. Spofforth, F. Allen, D. Gregory, W. Midwinter, T. Garrett, H. Boyle.

3
W. L. Murdoch, Australia's captain in five series, later played for England against South Africa.

4
George Ulyett, England's all-rounder in the first series.

1

2

J. Blackham   T. Horan   F. R. Spofforth   F. E. Allen   G. H. Bailey   D. W. Gregory   J. Conway (Manager)   W. Midwinter   A. Bannerman   T. W. Garrett   C. Bannerman   H. F. Boyle   W. L. Murdoch

THE AUSTRALIAN CRICKET TEAM

3

4

1882
The Ashes

On August 30, 1882 the following notice appeared among the obituaries in the London *Sporting Times*:

'In affectionate remembrance of English Cricket which died at the Oval, 29th August, 1882. Deeply lamented by a large circle of sorrowing friends and acquaintances. R.I.P.

N.B. The body will be cremated and the Ashes taken to Australia.'

England had suffered her first home defeat (having in 1880 comfortably won the only previous Test in England), but the margin was only seven runs after a fluctuating game played in appalling conditions.

England had bowled Australia out for 63 in the first innings, but did little better when they batted, reaching only 101. In their second innings Australia managed 122, but there was an unfortunate incident in which W. G. Grace threw down the wicket of the number eight Jones while he was patting the pitch: Jones was given out, but the Australians wanted revenge. England needed only 85 to win and reached 51 with only 2 wickets down. But then 'The Demon' Spofforth made the most of the damp wicket, finishing with 7 for 44 in England's total of 77 (Grace 32). His match figures of 14 for 90 were not bettered by an Australian bowler against England until Massie's sixteen wickets at Lords ninety years later.

The urn containing the Ashes now stays at Lords. It was presented to the England captain the next year at Melbourne after England had won two consecutive Tests and is said to contain the ashes of a bail.

1882-96
England on Top

Between 1877 and 1912 there were ninety-four England–Australia Tests: England won forty, Australia thirty-five and nineteen were drawn. There were Tests either in England or Australia most years, for South Africa was the only other Test-playing country, playing England for the first time in 1888 and Australia in 1902.

Australia had a lean spell from 1885 to 1888, losing seven consecutive Tests to England, three of them by an innings. The most remarkable of these was at Sydney on the 1886–87 tour, when C. T. B. Turner and J. J. Ferris (both

5
The score-card of the first official Test match between Australia and England, played at Melbourne Cricket Ground on March 15, 16 and 17, 1877.

---

5 AUSTRALIA

Batsman			1st			2nd
C. Bannerman	retired hurt	165		b Ulyett	4
N. Thompson	b Hill	1		c Emmett b Shaw	7
T. P. Horan	c Hill b Shaw	12		c Selby b Ulyett	20
D. W. Gregory	run out	1		b Shaw	3
B. B. Cooper	b Southerton	15		b Shaw	3
W. E. Midwinter	c Ulyett b Southerton	5		c Southerton b Ulyett	17
E. J. Gregory	c Greenwood b Lillywhite	0		c Emmett b Ulyett	11
J. M. Blackham	b Southerton	17		lbw Shaw	6
T. W. Garrett	not out	18		c Emmett b Shaw	0
T. Kendall	c Southerton b Shaw	3		not out	17
J. Hodges	b Shaw	0		b Lillywhite	8
Extras	(b 4, lb 2, w 2)	8		(b 5, lb 3)	8
Total		**245**		**Total**	**104**

ENGLAND

Batsman			1st			2nd
H. Jupp	lbw Garrett	63		lbw Midwinter	4
J. Selby	c Cooper b Hodges	7		c Horan b Hodges	38
H. R. J. Charlwood	c Blackham b Midwinter	36		b Kendall	13
G. Ulyett	lbw Thompson	10		b Kendall	24
A. Greenwood	c E. Gregory b Midwinter	1		c Midwinter b Kendall	5
T. Armitage	c Blackham b Midwinter	9		c Blackham b Kendall	3
A. Shaw	b Midwinter	10		st Blackham b Kendall	2
T. Emmett	b Midwinter	8		b Kendall	9
A. Hill	not out	35		c Thompson b Kendall	0
James Lillywhite	c and b Kendall	10		b Hodges	4
J. Southerton	c Cooper b Garrett	6		not out	1
Extras	(lb 1)	1		(b 4, lb 1)	5
Total		**196**		**Total**	**108**

FALL OF WICKETS
AUSTRALIA

Wkt	1st	2nd
1st	2	7
2nd	40	27
3rd	41	31
4th	118	31
5th	142	35
6th	143	58
7th	197	97
8th	243	75
9th	245	75
10th	—	104

ENGLAND

Wkt	1st	2nd
1st	23	0
2nd	79	7
3rd	98	20
4th	109	22
5th	121	62
6th	130	68
7th	145	92
8th	145	93
9th	168	100
10th	196	108

UMPIRES:
CURTIS A. REID,
B. TERRY

ENGLAND	1st Innings				2nd Innings			
	O	M	R	W	O	M	R	W
Shaw	55.3	34	51	3	34	16	38	5
Hill	23	10	42	1	14	6	18	0
Ulyett	25	12	36	0	19	7	39	4
Southerton	37	11	61	3				
Armitage	3	0	15	0				
Lillywhite	14	5	19	1	1	0	1	1
Emmett	12	7	13	0				

AUSTRALIA	1st Innings				2nd Innings			
	O	M	R	W	O	M	R	W
Hodges	9	0	27	1	7	5	7	2
Garrett	18.1	10	22	2	2	0	9	0
Kendall	38	16	54	1	33.1	12	55	7
Midwinter	54	21	78	5	19	7	23	1
Thompson	17	10	14	1				
D. W. Gregory					5	1	9	0

6
The victorious Australian tourists of 1882.
Back row: S. Jones, A. Bannerman,
G. Bonnor, F. Spofforth, J. Blackham,
G. Palmer, G. Giffen, T. Garrett, H. Massie,
P. McDonnell. *Seated:* W. Murdoch,
H. Boyle, T. Horan.

7
F. R. Spofforth, the Demon Bowler, as
seen by contemporary cartoonist Spy.

playing in their first Test) bowled
unchanged through the England
first innings of 45, which is still
England's lowest score against
Australia. But even then England
won the match by 13 runs. Turner
was nicknamed 'The Terror':
although he may not be well
known today, his record in Tests
between the two countries is
supreme. He took 101 wickets
with fast off-cutters in only seventeen Tests: his average of 16·53
runs per wicket is better than that
of any of the other ten bowlers on
both sides to have taken 100
wickets or more. (In two Tests
in 1890 he opened the batting as
well as the bowling, but with less
success.)

There was another amazing Test
at Sydney eight years later when
England again won, this time after
being forced to follow on. Syd
Gregory, who was later to captain
Australia, played one of the great
innings of Test cricket in
Australia's first innings: going in
sixth, he made 201 and added 154
in only 73 minutes for the ninth
wicket with Blackham—a record

7

8

8
W. G. Grace, the most famous of all
pre-First World War cricketers.

9

9
Lord Harris, England captain in three of
the early series.

which still stands. But the second innings was a different story: on a wet wicket Australia could not cope with the slow left arm of Bobby Peel (6 for 67) and England won by ten runs.

Peel was to have an even finer hour at the Oval in 1896 in W. G. Grace's last Test as Captain. England had won at Lords, but Australia won a memorable game at Old Trafford. This has often

been called 'Richardson's match' because of the heroic three-hour spell by the great Surrey fast bowler. But the wicket keeper Kelly, partnered by the number eight Trumble, saw Australia home to a three wicket victory.

So the series depended on the final Test at the Oval. England's chances were seemingly ruined before the start by the first instance of industrial action in

Tests–five players went on strike for £20 instead of the £10 offered. On the last day of the Test Australia needed only 111 to win, but again the weather came to England's aid. On a sticky wicket Australia were dismissed for 44, Peel taking 6 for 23 and the medium-paced J. T. Hearne 4 for 19.

1897-98 Clem Hill and Joe Darling

This was the first series in which Australia completely outplayed England, winning four Tests to one. England won the first Test, but G. H. S. Trott led Australia to victories by an innings in each of the next two. Then at Melbourne the 21-year-old from Adelaide, Clem Hill, scored 188 out of the first-innings total of 323 after Australia had at one stage lost six wickets for 58. Australia went on to win by eight wickets. Clem Hill was possibly the greatest left hander of all time. He played forty-one times against England between 1896 and 1912, when he was captain, scoring 2660 runs – more than any other Australian except Bradman. He scored four hundreds, one of them at Sheffield in under two hours, and he still holds the record for the eighth wicket – 243 with Hartigan at Adelaide in 1908. He also caught the crucial catch in the Old Trafford Test of 1902 – one of the closest Tests ever played, as we shall see.

The other hero of this series was Joe Darling, also from Adelaide, who scored three centuries. His 160 in the second innings of the final Test at Sydney won the game for Australia, who had been 96 behind on the first innings.

10

11

10
Captain in the 1890s, Harry Trott was one of Australia's best all-rounders.

11
Left-hand all-rounder Bobby Peel toured Australia four times.

12
A. E. Stoddart took over the England captaincy from W. G. Grace, on two tours to Australia.

13
Tom Richardson took five or more Australian wickets in an innings eleven times between 1893 and 1898.

14
William Gunn and Arthur Shrewsbury, Nottinghamshire and England batsmen of the 1880s and 1890s.

1902
The Closest
Tests of All

Between the first Test in Sydney of that 1897–98 tour and the start of Australia's tour to England in 1902, England had won only one Test while Australia had won nine.

The series of 1902, however, was fought tooth and nail between two of the strongest sides ever to take the field. The following played during the series:

England: A. C. MacLaren (capt.), T. W. Hayward, C. B. Fry, S. F. Barnes, W. Rhodes, G. L. Jessop, G. H. Hirst, L. C. Braund, A. A. Lilley, Hon F. S. Jackson, J. T. Tyldesley, R. Abel, W. H. Lockwood, L. C. H. Palairet, K. S. Ranjitsinhji, F. W. Tate.

Australia: J. Darling (capt.), C. Hill, V. T. Trumper, H. Trumble, A. J. Hopkins, M. A. Noble, R. A. Duff, S. E. Gregory, W. W. Armstrong, J. J. Kelly, J. V. Saunders, E. Jones, W. P. Howell.

Several on each side would be in anybody's selection of the best elevens over 100 years.

After two rain-affected draws,

15
Archie MacLaren, England's captain in the thrilling 1902 series.

16
Gilbert Jessop's match-winning century at the Oval in 1902 was the fastest in matches between the countries.

17
A page from a 1902 magazine showing incidents of the first Test. *Centre:* MacLaren is run out. *Clockwise from top left:* Australia's procession to and from the wicket; the conditions; Fry out for a duck; F. S. Jackson; inspecting the wicket; spectators; using the sawdust; Jones drops Tyldesley.

16

15

Australia won the third Test by 143 runs. Then came the famous Old Trafford Test. On the first morning on a rain-sodden ground Trumper scored a century before lunch – the first ever in a Test. But Lockwood, recalled to Test cricket after a period when he had been dropped by his county Surrey, took 6 for 48 thus limiting Australia's first-innings lead to 27. In their second innings Lockwood bowled even better, partnered by Wilfred Rhodes. Australia were three wickets down for only ten when their captain Joe Darling came in to play a match-winning innings. He was dropped in the deep at 17 by the luckless Fred Tate, playing in his one and only Test, and went on to make 37 out of the Australian total of 86. Lockwood had taken another 5 wickets for 28. So England needed 124 to win. With 68 on the board for the loss of only 2 wickets they were well on the way; even with 4 down for 92 victory seemed

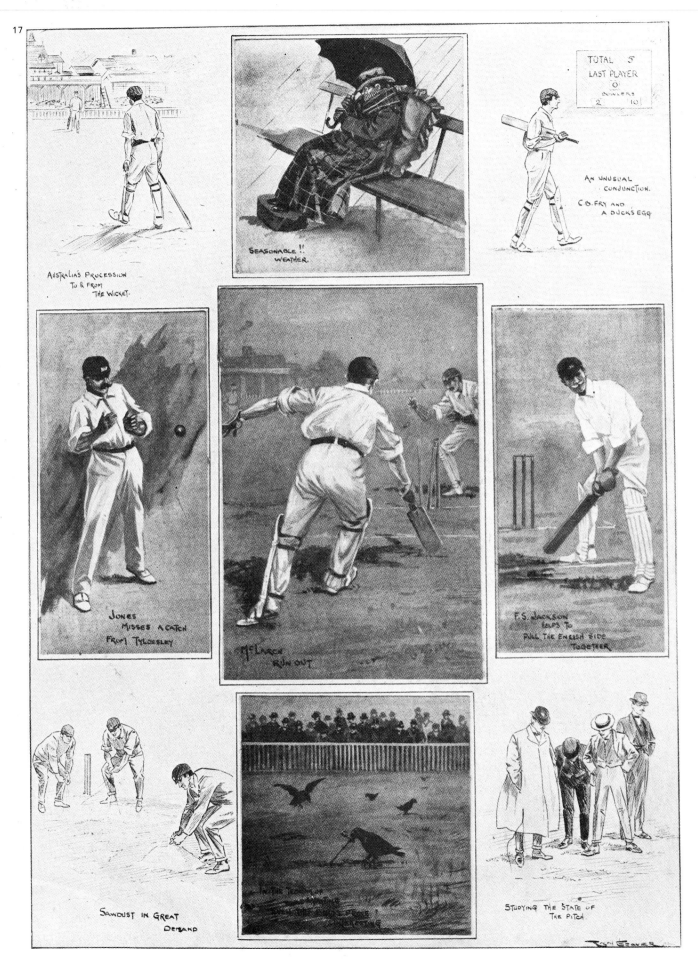

AUSTRALIA'S PROCESSION
TO & FROM
THE WICKET.

SEASONABLE !!
WEATHER.

TOTAL 5
LAST PLAYER 0
BOWLERS
2 10

AN UNUSUAL
CONJUNCTION.
C.B.FRY AND
A DUCK'S EGG

JONES
MISSES A CATCH
FROM TYLDESLEY

McLAREN
RUN OUT

F.S. JACKSON
HELPS TO
PULL THE ENGLISH SIDE
TOGETHER

SAWDUST IN GREAT
DEMAND

STUDYING THE STATE OF
THE PITCH

assured. But then wickets fell regularly, the ninth, that of wicket-keeper Lilley, with England still eight runs short. This wicket fell to Clem Hill's magnificent catch in the outfield, when he sprinted thirty yards to hold the catch one-handed and save what looked like four critical runs. Then rain stopped play for forty minutes before poor Tate was bowled and England had lost by three runs.

Incredibly, the final Test at the Oval was equally exciting. In this his last Test Lockwood took 5 for 45 in Australia's second innings of 121, leaving England 263 to win. At 48 for 5 it looked like a certain Australian victory, but Gilbert Jessop, cricket's mightiest hitter, scored 104 in seventy-five minutes and F. S. Jackson stayed at the other end to make 49 and put England within sight of an improbable win. But there were still fifteen needed as Wilfred Rhodes came in to join his fellow-Yorkshireman George Hirst, who then gave him the famous advice 'We'll get them by singles'—and they did. So England had won by one wicket.

18
George Hirst helped fellow Yorkshireman Rhodes "get them by singles" at the Oval in 1902. A Spy cartoon.

19
The Australian captain in 1902 was Joe Darling.

AUSTRALIA

					FALL OF WICKETS

Batsman	1st Innings		2nd Innings	
V. T. Trumper	b Hirst	42	run out	2
R. A. Duff	c Lilley b Hirst	23	b Lockwood	6
C. Hill	b Hirst	11	c MacLaren b Hirst	34
J. Darling	c Lilley b Hirst	3	c MacLaren b Lockwood	15
M. A. Noble	c and b Jackson	52	b Braund	13
S. E. Gregory	b Hirst	23	b Braund	9
W. W. Armstrong	b Jackson	17	b Lockwood	21
A. J. Hopkins	c MacLaren b Lockwood	40	c Lilley b Lockwood	3
H. Trumble	not out	64	not out	7
J. J. Kelly	c Rhodes b Braund	39	lbw Lockwood	0
J. V. Saunders	lbw Braund	0	c Tyldesley b Rhodes	2
Extras	(b 5, lb 3, nb 2)	10	(b 7, lb 2)	9
Total		**324**	**Total**	**121**

FALL OF WICKETS

AUSTRALIA

Wkt	1st	2nd
1st	47	6
2nd	63	9
3rd	69	31
4th	82	71
5th	126	75
6th	174	91
7th	175	99
8th	256	114
9th	324	115
10th	324	121

ENGLAND

Batsman	1st Innings		2nd Innings	
A. C. MacLaren	c Armstrong b Trumble	10	b Saunders	2
L. C. H. Palairet	b Trumble	20	b Saunders	6
J. T. Tyldesley	b Trumble	33	b Saunders	0
T. Hayward	b Trumble	0	c Kelly b Saunders	7
Hon F. S. Jackson	c Armstrong b Saunders	2	c and b Trumble	49
L. C. Braund	c Hill b Trumble	22	c Kelly b Trumble	2
G. L. Jessop	b Trumble	13	c Noble b Armstrong	104
G. H. Hirst	c and b Trumble	43	not out	58
W. H. Lockwood	c Noble b Saunders	25	lbw Trumble	2
A. A. Lilley	c Trumper b Trumble	0	c Darling b Trumble	16
W. Rhodes	not out	0	not out	6
Extras	(b 13, lb 2)	15	(b 5, lb 6)	11
Total		**183**	**Total (9 wkts)**	**263**

ENGLAND

Wkt	1st	2nd
1st	31	5
2nd	36	5
3rd	62	10
4th	67	31
5th	67	48
6th	83	157
7th	137	187
8th	179	214
9th	183	248
10th	183	—

UMPIRES:
C. E. RICHARDSON,
A. A. WHITE

ENGLAND	1st Innings				2nd Innings			
	O	M	R	W	O	M	R	W
Lockwood	24	2	85	1	20	6	45	5
Rhodes	29	9	46	0	22	7	38	1
Hirst	29	5	77	5	5	1	7	1
Braund	16.5	5	29	2	9	1	15	2
Jackson	20	4	66	2	5	3	7	0
Jessop	6	2	11	0				

AUSTRALIA	1st Innings				2nd Innings			
	O	M	R	W	O	M	R	W
Trumble	31	13	65	8	33.5	4	108	4
Saunders	23	7	79	2	24	3	105	4
Noble	7	3	24	0	5	0	11	0
Armstrong					4	0	28	1

1903-04
Australia 2
England 3

When 'Plum' Warner set off with his team for Australia he was given no chance of recovering the Ashes. But he was a superb captain and a supreme optimist. Even he could not have expected, though, that R. E. Foster would score 287 in his very first Test, the first of the series, at Sydney. But he did, thereby setting a world Test record, which stood for twenty-six years. In the same match Noble, captaining Australia for the first time, scored 133 and Trumper 185 not out, coming in at a time when Australia still needed over 100 to avoid an innings defeat with three wickets down. This match also saw the first riot in Test cricket, when a section of the crowd threw bottles after Clem Hill had been given run out. After all this, England won by 5 wickets.

They won the next Test at Melbourne, too – this time by 185 runs, thanks largely to Wilfred Rhodes, who took 15 wickets in the match for 124: of English bowlers only Laker has ever taken more wickets in a Test against Australia. Australia won the Adelaide Test easily after centuries by Trumper and Syd Gregory.

The decisive fourth Test at Sydney was settled by the remarkable bowling of B. J. T. Bosanquet, the inventor of the googly. This was his first Test series and the great Australian batsmen could make little of his strange style. His 6 for 51 in the second innings won the match.

This wonderful series ended with the most convincing win of the series – by Australia, whose margin was 218 runs. Hugh Trumble, the Melbourne medium-pacer, took 7 for 28 on his home ground to add to the 4 for 107 and 5 for 34 he had taken in the second Test there. Most remarkable, though, was the fact that he achieved a hat-trick with the last three balls he bowled – his last three in Test cricket. He thus became the only man who has ever achieved two hat-tricks in Tests, for he had also taken the last three wickets off consecutive balls in the Test of January, 1902.

20

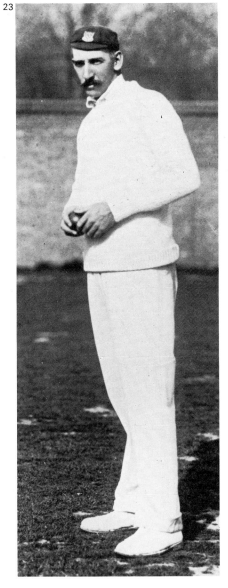

23

24

25

26

22
Prince Ranjitsinhji (Cambridge) and C. B. Fry (Oxford) were on opposite sides in the 1893 University match but played together for Sussex and England.

23
Hugh Trumble, the only man to achieve two hat-tricks against England.

24
Australia's prolific batsman of pre-First World War days, Clem Hill.

25
Syd Gregory, of the famous cricketing family, at 5 ft 5 in (164 cm) was the smallest player to represent Australia.

26
Australia's finest batsman before the First World War, the immortal Victor Trumper.

1905-14 The Golden Age of Cricket Ends

It is not surprising that the period from the 1890s to the outbreak of the First World War is termed The Golden Age of Cricket: there were so many great players and so many great games.

The series in England in 1905 belonged to one man, who alas never played a Test in Australia – the England captain, the Honourable F. S. Jackson, later an M.P. and Governor of Bengal. He had scored 91 in his first Test in 1893, but now as captain he did everything. He won the toss in all five Tests; he topped the England batting averages with 70·28, having scored two centuries, an 82 and a 76 and scored more runs in the series than anyone on either side; and he topped the England bowling averages with 13 wickets at 15·46 each. England won two Tests to nil and had the better of three draws.

With that, Jackson retired from first-class cricket, no doubt much to the relief of the Australians, who went on to win the next series in 1907–8 decisively by four Tests to one. The highlight of that series was the record eighth wicket stand at Adelaide between Clem Hill and Hartigan, already mentioned. Australia won that Test by 245 runs, but they did even better in the next one at Melbourne, where they won by 308 runs. Australia completely outplayed England throughout the series except in the second Test, which England narrowly won. Trumper scored 166 at Sydney and Warwick Armstrong scored 133 not out at Melbourne – his first century against England, though he was to reach his peak when captain after the First World War. Australia were also indebted to the consistent left arm bowling of Saunders (9 for 104 in the fourth Test), supported by Cotter, O'Connor, Noble and Macartney, who were too much for England, despite the inclusion of a promising newcomer by the name of J. B.

27

28

Hobbs, then aged 25.

Australia remained on top in England in 1909; this time their captain Monty Noble won the toss all five times. Much of the credit for Australia's success in these years belongs to Noble, a Sydney dentist when not on the cricket field. He did the double of a thousand runs and a hundred wickets in Tests in only 27 Tests:

27
The record number of dismissals by an English wicket-keeper of 84, achieved by Arthur Lilley before 1909, still stood when the Centenary Test Match began 68 years later.

28
A googly is sometimes called a Bosie after its inventor B. J. T. Bosanquet.

29
R. E. Foster, whose 287 at Sydney in 1903 is the highest score made in a Test debut.

30
Tom Hayward, prolific Surrey and England opening batsman of the turn of the century.

31
Everything went right for England's captain, the Honourable F. S. Jackson in 1905.

he took more English wickets than any other Australian bowler except Trumble; he was a great close fielder; his captaincy was so highly rated that C. B. Fry named him as captain of an all-time 'Earth XI' to play Mars!

Australia won that 1909 series by two Tests to one, but the final Test was only saved by Warren Bardsley who scored a hundred in each innings – a feat only repeated by Arthur Morris in Tests against England. Apart from Noble's captaincy, the main credit for winning the series belongs to Australia's bowlers – Cotter, Laver (8 for 31 in the first innings at

Manchester), Macartney and Armstrong.

It was in Australia in 1911–12 that Hobbs established himself as one of the truly great batsmen. He scored centuries in both the Melbourne Tests and 187 at Adelaide to help England win all three: then England won the final Test at Sydney (the young Frank Woolley scoring 133 not out), making it four in a row after Australia had won the first Test. In later years Hobbs was to become a perfectionist: those who saw him before the First World War describe him as a defiant if somewhat risky stroke-maker. In

all he was to play forty-one Tests against Australia between 1907 and 1930, scoring 3636 runs at an average of 54·26. No other Englishman has scored as many as

3000 runs against Australia—of Australians only Bradman has exceeded Hobbs's total.

It was on this 1911–12 tour that the Melbourne crowd gave the

32
The 1909 Australians. *Top row:* S. E. Gregory, W. J. Whitty, J. A. O'Connor, W. W. Armstrong. *Second row:* F. Laver, W. Carkeek, H. Carter, A. J. Hopkins. *Bottom row:* W. Bardsley, V. S. Ransford, M. A. Noble (captain), V. T. Trumper.

England captain J. W. H. T. Douglas his nickname, noting his initials and irritated by his slow scoring – 'Johnny Won't Hit To-Day'. He was well served by two fine bowlers on this tour, S. F. Barnes and F. R. Foster, who shared sixty-six of the ninety-five Australian wickets that fell. The heaviest English win of the series was in the fourth Test at Melbourne, which was nearly called off because of labour unrest which threatened a general strike. But the game started, Douglas won the toss and surprisingly put Australia in: Barnes and Foster bowled them out for 191. Then, when England batted, Hobbs and Rhodes (number eleven in 1902 but now an opener) put on 323 for the first wicket. This still stands as the record opening stand in England–Australia Tests. England amassed 589 runs; then Syd Barnes had one of his finest hours in twenty Tests against Australia, taking the first five Australian wickets for six runs, including

33
Syd Barnes took five or more Australian wickets in an innings a record twelve times.

34
Sir Pelham Warner captained England when the Ashes were regained in 1903–04.

34

those of Bardsley, Hill and Armstrong. Australia struggled to 173, losing by an innings and 225 runs.

The demoralized Australians had suffered throughout the series from selectorial wrangles, which ended in fisticuffs between Clem Hill, who in this series had captained Australia for the first time, and a non-playing fellow-selector called McAlister. To make matters worse, the Australian Board of Control were not able to offer sufficiently attractive terms for the tour to England later in 1912 to contest the 'Triangular Tests'. This was the only series of full-length Tests ever held between more than two countries. England, Australia and South Africa each played one another three times. But the series is best forgotten. Six of Australia's leading players refused to tour because of the terms, which resulted in probably the weakest Australian touring side of all time leaving for England under the captaincy of the surprised Syd Gregory, outstanding batsman and

33

veteran of over fifty Tests, but no captain. South Africa were even weaker, Australia beating them twice. Moreover, it was a wet summer. England convincingly won the only Test completed against Australia but the only people to distinguish themselves in this Oval Test were the 36-year-old Syd Barnes with 5 for 30 in the first Australian innings and, for Australia, Hazlitt with 7 for 25 in England's second innings.

1920-21
Armstrong and Australia unbeaten

Warwick Armstrong was a giant of a man in every respect. He was 6 ft 3 in (190 cm) tall and by the time he took over the captaincy of Australia in 1920 at the age of forty-one he was well over 20 stone (127 kg). He had played in thirty-two Tests against England since 1901 and had had his famous days both with bat and ball. But he will be best remembered for the two series against England when he was captain, those of 1920–21 in Australia and 1921 in England. He led Australia to victory in eight Tests out of ten, the other two being drawn. Certainly he had some fine players, but he was a shrewd and forceful captain, who led by example, scoring three dazzling hundreds in the 1920–21 series. All five Tests of that series were won by huge margins with only Jack Hobbs offering any real resistance, with 122 in the second Test and 123 in the third. The men who bowled England out were J. M. Gregory, E. A. McDonald and A. A. Mailey. In his use of Gregory and McDonald, Armstrong was able to demoralize the English batsmen by sheer pace operating from both ends –then a new concept in Tests. With his captain's encouragement, Gregory also bowled bumpers, which resulted in hostile reactions from the English crowds in 1921. Perhaps it was the knowledge of Armstrong's success with Gregory and McDonald that led to Douglas Jardine's bodyline tactics with Larwood and Voce twelve years later. Exceptional pace can demoralize the best of batsmen and in itself wins matches, as we have seen in the last few seasons with Lillee and Thomson for Australia and Roberts and Holding for West Indies.

Armstrong's third ace bowler was Arthur Mailey, a complete contrast with his leg-breaks and unreadable googlies. In the 1920–21 series, his first in Test cricket, he took thirty-six wickets, more than any Australian has ever taken in a series against England: what is more, because of injury, he did not bowl at all in the second Test at Melbourne. However, in the fourth, again at Melbourne, he showed what he might have done by taking 9 for 121 in England's second innings – and having the tenth man dropped.

In the 1920–21 series Australia's runs were scored by Armstrong, H. L. Collins, Pellew, Kelleway and Macartney. In the second Test Gregory scored 100 exactly and then took 7 wickets for 69 in England's first innings. Gregory made another notable contribution

to Australia's sweeping victory by holding 15 catches in the series, mostly in the slips; this still stands as the world record for catches in a series, excluding wicket-keepers. One final most necessary ingredient of Australia's success was an able wicket-keeper, essential with Mailey in the side. During the series the most successful of all Australian wicket-keepers, Bert Oldfield, shared the wicket keeping duties with the veteran Carter. By the time he retired in 1936, he had made ninety dismissals in thirty-eight Tests against England. Many would regard him as the greatest 'keeper of all.

Helped by exceptionally dry conditions in England in 1921, Armstrong's side won the first three Tests in much the same fashion as they had the last five in Australia. Gregory and MacDonald destroyed England in the first Test at Nottingham. Curiously, the only Australian century of the series was Macartney's in the third Test at Leeds – but Australia did not need all that many runs to beat England in 1921: the disarray of England is shown by the fact that no fewer than thirty players played for them during the series. Armstrong's Test career finished with two drawn games, the final match at the Oval being such a dull affair as Mead slowly made his 182 not out that Armstrong retired to the outfield where, to the fury of the crowd, he read a newspaper.

35
Maurice Tate, holder of the record for the most wickets taken in a series in Australia (38 in 1924–25).

36
Sir Donald Bradman in 1926 – an eighteen-year-old starting his incomparable career.

1924-29 Honours Even Over Three Series

Arthur Gilligan captained the England side to Australia in 1924–5. Despite the fact that Armstrong had retired, his successor H. L. Collins still managed to lead Australia to four victories to England's one. There were three new faces in his side who were to make a considerable impact on Test cricket. W. H. Ponsford scored 110 in his first Test innings: he was to score

another four against England and provide a fine partner for Bradman in his heyday. Victor Richardson scored 138 in the first innings of his second Test and caught a superb catch to dismiss Gilligan at the Adelaide Oval in the next Test, enabling Australia to achieve a narrow victory. Now the road leading to the Adelaide Oval is named after him. He gave Australia the start they needed in

most of the nineteen Tests in which he played. Recently his two grandsons, Ian and Greg Chappell have led Australia in Tests.

The third newcomer in 1924–25 was Clarrie Grimmett, the steadiest of all leg-break bowlers. He came into the side only for the last match at Sydney, where he took 11 for 82. By the time he retired in 1935 he had achieved the record number of wickets in all

Tests (216), which was to stand till Lindwall for Australia and Bedser for England broke it. 106 of these wickets were taken in Tests against England – a total still exceeded by only three Australians. The final Australian who should be mentioned for this series is Jack Ryder, who made a magnificent 201 not out in the Adelaide Test after six wickets had fallen for 119. Later he was to captain Australia and later still was a selector for many years.

Despite losing the series so heavily, England too had their moments. Hobbs scored centuries in the first three Tests, all of which England were to lose. His new opening partner was a 30-year-old Yorkshireman, Herbert Sutcliffe: their partnerships over the next four series laid the foundation for England's Test recuperation.

Sutcliffe's arrival on the Test scene was dramatic: 59 and 115 in the first Test, followed by 176 and 127 in the second. The latter lasted into the seventh day and Sutcliffe was on the field for all but eighty-six minutes of the match – nearly twenty-eight hours in all. No other Englishman has scored three centuries in consecutive Test innings. Finally, there was Maurice Tate, son of Fred Tate, who had played in that famous Manchester Test of 1902. Tate was one of the very finest of all fast-medium bowlers. He took eleven wickets in his first Test and nine in his second and ended the series breaking Mailey's recent record by taking a total of 38 wickets. This is still the record number of wickets in a series in Australia and has only been bettered for England by Laker and Bedser.

The final two series of the 1920s saw a revival in English fortunes, for they won both – the 1926 series in the final Test after four draws and the 1928–29 series convincingly by four victories to one. Hobbs scored another two hundreds in 1926 and, with Sutcliffe (161) ensured in their second innings that England won the final Oval

36

Test to take the series. This series saw the final Test appearances of two Australian stalwarts, Warren Bardsley and C. G. Macartney, aged forty-three and forty respectively: they went out in a blaze of glory, despite losing the series. Bardsley carried his bat at Lords for 193 in Australia's first-innings total of 383. Macartney if anything outshone Bardsley, scoring three centuries during the series. The finest was at Leeds where he came in to face the second ball of the match after Bardsley had been out first ball (this in the Test immediately following his triumph at Lords). Macartney proceeded to score a hundred before lunch, a feat only previously achieved by Trumper, and went on to make 151.

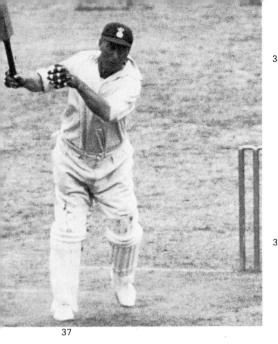

Both had retired from Test cricket by the time Percy Chapman took England to Australia in 1928–29 to face Jack Ryder's Australians.

But the brightest star of all made his first appearance that year – Don Bradman, a twenty-year-old from Bowral, New South Wales. His major achievements of course followed in the 1930s, but in this series his innings of 112 and 123 in the two Melbourne Tests gave an indication of what lay ahead for English bowlers. Woodfull scored three centuries in the series to add to the two he had scored in England in 1926; 19-year-old A. A. Jackson made a brilliant 164 at Adelaide; Kippax, Ryder and Hendry also scored centuries during the series. But England were still too good for Australia, with their new star, Wally Hammond, also in his first series, making even more of an impact than Bradman. He scored 251 in England's only innings at Sydney in the second Test, 200 and 32 in the third at Melbourne and then 119 not out and 177 at Adelaide in the fourth Test. With the bowling of Tate, Harold Larwood, George Geary and J. C. White (who took thirteen wickets at Adelaide) and Hobbs, Hendren, Leyland and Sutcliffe also scoring runs perhaps it is not surprising that England had so much the better of this series. By 1930, however, Bradman was in full flight.

37
Philip Mead made 182 not out at the Oval in 1921.

38
Arthur Gilligan captained England in Australia, 1924–25.

39
Wilfred Rhodes, one of England's greatest all-rounders.

40
The brilliant Australian batsman, Archie Jackson, died aged 24 on the brink of a great career.

41
Ernest Tyldesley, who many thought should have played more than five times against Australia.

AUSTRALIA

W. M. Woodfull	....	b Hammond	50
A. A. Jackson	......	c Larwood b Tate	1
D. G. Bradman	.....	c Duckworth b Tate	334
A. F. Kippax	....	c Chapman b Tate	77
S. J. McCabe	.....	b Larwood	30
V. Y. Richardson	....	c Larwood b Tate	1
E. L. A'Beckett	.....	c Chapman b Geary	29
W. A. Oldfield	......	c Hobbs b Tate	2
C. V. Grimmett	.....	c Duckworth b Tyldesley ..	24
T. W. Wall	....	b Tyldesley	3
P. M. Hornibrook	....	not out	1
Extras	....	(b 5, lb 8, w 1)	14
Total	....	....	**566**

ENGLAND

J. B. Hobbs	....	c A'Beckett b Grimmett	29	run out 13
H. Sutcliffe	....	c Hornibrook b Grimmett ...	32	not out 28
W. R. Hammond	....	c Oldfield b McCabe	113	c Oldfield b Grimmett .. 35
K. S. Duleepsinhji	....	b Hornibrook	35	c Grimmett b Hornibrook 10
M. Leyland	....	c Kippax b Wall	44	not out 1
G. Geary	....	run out	0	
G. Duckworth	......	c Oldfield b A'Beckett	33	
A. P. F. Chapman	....	b Grimmett	45	
M. W. Tate	....	c Jackson b Grimmett	22	
H. Larwood	....	not out	10	
R. Tyldesley	....	c Hornibrook b Grimmett ..	6	
Extras	....	(b 9, lb 10, nb 3)	22	(lb 8) 8
Total	....	....	**391**	**Total (3 wkts)** **95**

FALL OF WICKETS

AUSTRALIA

Wkt	1st	2nd
1st	2	—
2nd	194	—
3rd	423	—
4th	486	—
5th	491	—
6th	508	—
7th	519	—
8th	544	—
9th	565	—
10th	566	—

ENGLAND

Wkt	1st	2nd
1st	53	24
2nd	64	74
3rd	123	94
4th	206	—
5th	206	—
6th	289	—
7th	319	—
8th	370	—
9th	375	—
10th	391	—

UMPIRES:
W. BESTWICK,
T. W. OATES

ENGLAND *1st Innings*

	O	M	R	W
Larwood	33	3	139	1
Tate	39	9	124	5
Geary	35	10	95	1
Tyldesley	33	5	104	2
Hammond	17	3	46	1
Leyland	11	0	44	0

AUSTRALIA

	1st Innings				2nd Innings			
	O	M	R	W	O	M	R	W
Wall	40	12	70	1	10	3	20	0
A'Beckett	28	8	47	1	11	4	19	0
Grimmett	56·2	16	135	5	17	3	33	1
Hornibrook	41	7	94	1	11·5	5	14	1
McCabe	10	4	23	1	2	1	1	0

43

42
The score-card of the third Test at Leeds in 1930.

43
England players of the 1920s and 1930s in a match at Scarborough, 1928. From left G. G. Macaulay, M. Leyland, G. Geary, A. P. F. Chapman, W. R. Hammond, G. Duckworth, E. Tyldesley, H. Sutcliffe, J. B. Hobbs, E. H. Hendren, M. W. Tate.

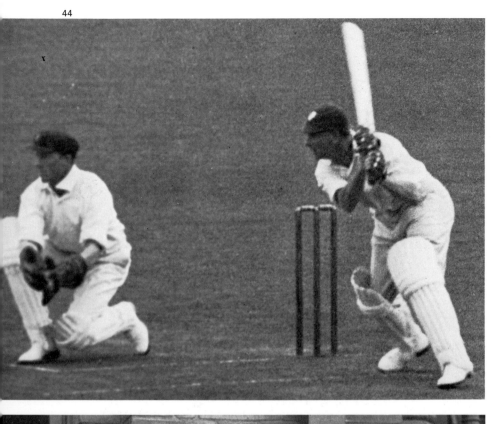

1930 England 1 Australia 2

Australia brought a young side to England in 1930 under Woodfull. In the first Test Australia were caught on a difficult wicket and were 126 behind on the first innings. Set to score 429 to win, Australia made a good try with Bradman getting 131, but were beaten by 93. At Lord's Duleepsinhji made 173 in an England total of 425, but Australia reached 585 before the third wicket fell (Woodfull 155, Bradman 254) and finally declared at their highest score of 729 for 6. Chapman scored a century in the second innings, but despite scoring 800 runs England were beaten by seven wickets.

At the end of the first day in the third Test at Leeds, Australia were 458 for 3, Bradman having given the most sustained display of batting power seen in Tests, scoring 300 in 5 hours 36 minutes. In all he made 334 of Australia's total of 566. A century by Hammond, rain and bad light saved England from defeat. Grimmett took five wickets for the fourth time in five innings.

Rain spoiled the fourth Test, and all was to play for at the Oval. England made 405 (Sutcliffe 161), but Australia passed this score with three men out and went on to 695. Ponsford made 110 and Bradman 232. England were dismissed for 251 for Australia to regain the Ashes.

Grimmett's 29 wickets was then a record for an Australian in England, but the tour belonged to Bradman, whose figures for the series have never been approached: 974 runs at an average of 139·14.

44
Sir Jack Hobbs batting in 1930. Bert Oldfield is the wicket-keeper.

45
England's most famous opening pair, Jack Hobbs and Herbert Sutcliffe.

46
Scenes of the first Test at Trent Bridge, 1930, from *The Illustrated London News*.

THE FIRST TEST MATCH: "SENSATIONS" OF ENGLAND v. AUSTRALIA.

THE DOMINANT AUSTRALIAN BOWLER: C. V. GRIMMETT IN ACTION DURING THE FIRST TEST MATCH.

A BOWLER WHO PROVED HIMSELF A FINE BAT: R. W. V. ROBINS IN ACTION.

THE GREAT ENGLAND BOWLER WHO HAD TO RETIRE ON ACCOUNT OF ILLNESS: LARWOOD IN ACTION.

THE FIRST TEST: THE SCENE DURING PLAY AT TRENT BRIDGE, NOTTINGHAM, IN THE MATCH WHICH ENGLAND WON BY 93 RUNS.

THE "BOY" BAT OF AUSTRALIA, THE ONLY CENTURY-MAKER OF THE MATCH: D. G. BRADMAN AT THE WICKET.

ENGLAND'S GREATEST BAT AND ENGLAND'S CAPTAIN FOR THE MATCH: HOBBS AND A. P. F. CHAPMAN.

HIT BY A BALL FROM WALL AND SO HURT THAT HE HAD TO RETIRE: SUTCLIFFE AT THE MOMENT OF THE ACCIDENT.

The first Test Match between England and Australia, played at Nottingham on June 13, 14, 16, and 17, provided cricket enthusiasts with numerous "sensations" after their own heart. On the first day Grimmett bowled remarkably well, and, in fact, dominated the game. On the second day Tate bowled Woodfull, who scored 2, Ponsford, who scored 3, and Bradman, who scored 8; Robins, who had scored 50 not out in England's first innings, won much praise as bowler; Chapman proved himself a great general; Hobbs completed his 1000 runs, the first Englishman to do so this season; and Hendren also completed his 1000. On the third day Hobbs and Sutcliffe, who had scored 78 and 29 respectively in England's first innings, scored 74 and 58. Hobbs was stumped, and Sutcliffe had to retire hurt, one of his thumbs having been damaged by a ball from Wall. On that day also Hendren made 72; and Grimmett and Wall were prominent. On the fourth day Larwood could not play, owing to gastritis, and Copley, of the Notts second eleven, was brought in as a substitute. Duleepsinhji, England's twelfth man, fielded in place of Sutcliffe. On that day also, Bradman scored 131 before being bowled by Robins. On the first day both teams wore black armlets as a mark of respect for the late Sir Frederick Toone, thrice manager of the teams sent to Australia by the M.C.C., and at lunch time flags were half-masted. England won by 93.

"DULEEP" PARALLELS A "RANJI" FEAT:

HIS FIRST TEST SUCCESS, AT LORD'S.

A. F. KIPPAX
(Australia).

C. V. GRIMMETT
(Australia).

W. M. WOODFULL
(Captain of Australia).

A. P. F. CHAPMAN
(Captain of England).

J. B. HOBBS
(England).

M. W. TATE
(England).

V. Y. RICHARDSON
(Australia).

E. HENDREN
(England).

W. H. PONSFORD
(Australia).

J. C. WHITE
(England).

W. A. OLDFIELD
(Australia).

W. R. HAMMOND
(England).

DULEEPSINHJI DROPPED AT SHORT LEG BY THE AUSTRALIAN CAPTAIN:
WOODFULL'S UNACCOUNTABLE LAPSE.

P. M. HORNIBROOK
(Australia).

G. O. ALLEN
(England).

A. FAIRFAX
(Australia).

DULEEPSINHJI'S FAMOUS LATE CUT: A SHOT THAT
ELUDED THE SLIP FIELDSMAN.

DULEEPSINHJI BADLY MISSED OFF A LATE
CUT BY WALL, IN THE SLIPS.

F. E. WOOLLEY
(England).

T. WALL
(Australia).

S. McCABE
(Australia).

D. G. BRADMAN
(Australia).

K. S. DULEEPSINHJI
(England).

G. DUCKWORTH
(England).

R. W. V. ROBINS
(England).

In England's first innings in the second Test Match, at Lord's, K. S. Duleepsinhji made 173 before being caught Bradman, bowled Grimmett; and thus very much more than justified his inclusion in the team. It was his first appearance for England in a Test Match against Australia, and his score was the highest ever made by a member of an England team against the Australians at Lord's. Duleepsinhji, our readers will no doubt recall, is a nephew of that great cricketer of other days, "Ranji," otherwise, H.H. the Jam Saheb of Nawanagar. "Ranji" was present at Lord's, and was, of course, one of the first to offer his congratulations. It is thirty-four years since he himself passed the century in his first Test Match against Australia, at Manchester. In the second innings Duleepsinhji scored 48, c. Oldfield, b. Hornibrook.

48

47
How *The Illustrated London News* saw Duleepsinhji's innings of 173 in the second Test at Lord's 1930.

48
England's controversial captain in the bodyline series, Douglas Jardine.

49
Woodfull ducks beneath a ball from Larwood at Brisbane on the 1932–33 bodyline tour.

1932-33 Australia 1 England 4

The 1932–33 series became known as the 'bodyline' series, and rivals the famous long count in the Dempsey–Tunney heavyweight title fight as an everlasting sporting controversy. Feelings were so bitter that after the third Test, when cables were exchanged between the two cricketing authorities, it seemed the tour might be abandoned. The English fast bowlers, particularly Larwood, bowled at the bodies of the Australian batsmen, with a ring of leg-side fielders ready to make catches as batsmen defended their bodies. It was a desperate measure born of frustration arising from plumb wickets and the dominance of Bradman, and it was ruthlessly carried out by new England captain Douglas Jardine.

Bradman was unfit for the first Test, in which Jack Fingleton and Bill O'Reilly made their debuts against England and Leslie Ames kept wicket for the first time against Australia. Australia scored 360, of which Stan McCabe made 187 not out in the finest innings played against bodyline. The Nawab of Pataudi made a century in his first Test, and with another from Hammond and 194 from Sutcliffe England made 524 and needed to score only one run in the second innings to win. Larwood took 5 for 96 and 5 for 28. Bradman returned for the second Test only to be bowled by Bill Bowes first ball, but he made 103 not out in the second innings and Australia won a low-scoring match by 111 runs. O'Reilly, this time, took five wickets in each innings.

The remaining Tests were all won by England, with Larwood being the chief destroyer of Australia. The incident which brought the bodyline anger to its height occurred in the third Test when Woodfull was hit over the heart by a ball from Larwood. He bravely batted on, and carried his bat for 73 not out in the second innings, but his understandably bitter remarks on bodyline led to the MCC offering to abandon the tour.

Eddie Paynter played a famous innings in the fourth Test, coming from hospital, where he was being

49

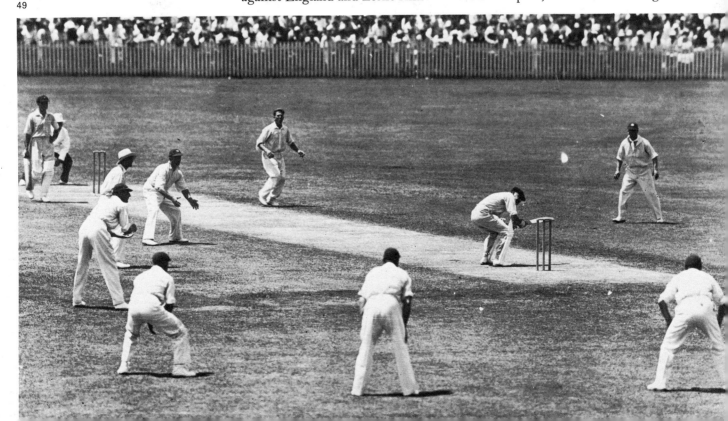

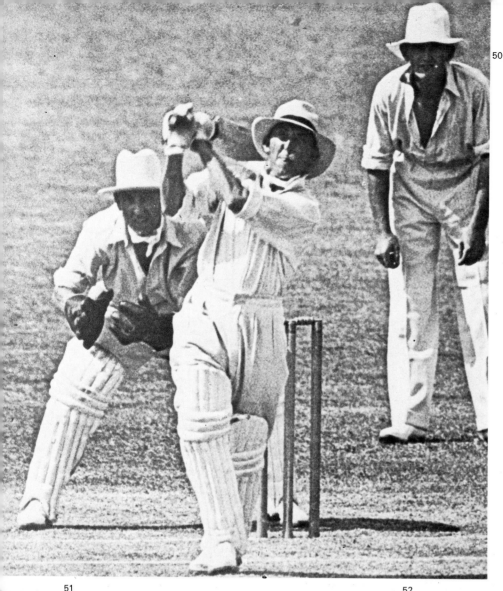

treated for tonsilitis, to score 83 and rescue England from difficulties. He won the Ashes with a six.

Larwood got a good reception from the Sydney crowd in the fifth Test when he scored 98 as a night watchman. Unfairly, he suffered most as a result of the bad feeling engendered by the tour, and did not play Test cricket again, and later he left England to live in Australia.

50
Eddie Paynter batting at Brisbane in 1933 when he made 83 when suffering from tonsilitis, and helped England win the Ashes.

51
W. M. Woodfull captained Australia on the tours of England in 1930 and 1934 and during the bodyline series of 1932–33.

52
Bill Ponsford shares two England v. Australia record partnerships (2nd and 4th wickets) with Bradman.

53
A striking photograph of the Nawab of Pataudi jumping out to drive.

54
Larwood's partner on the bodyline tour, Bill Voce went on to play against Australia after the war.

51

52

53

54

1934 England 1 Australia 2

The 1934 series resembled more that of 1930 than the bodyline series, with Bradman in his heaven and big scores being made. Australia won the first Test by 238, with A. G. Chipperfield having the misfortune to be out for 99 in his first Test match, and Ken Farnes, who was later killed in the war, getting five wickets in each innings of his first Test. England drew level in the second Test, when Maurice Leyland scored the first of three centuries in the series. Australia, chasing 440, were 192 for 2 when the third day's play began on a sticky wicket. Hedley Verity, also killed in the war, then took 14 wickets in a day (15 for 104 in the match) to skittle Australia for 284 and 118.

The third Test was drawn after England made 627 (Hendren 132, Leyland 153) and Australia 491 (McCabe 137). Bradman returned to his favourite Leeds for the fourth Test and scored 304, breaking the then record stand for any wicket between the countries by adding 388 with Ponsford for the fourth wicket. Rain saved England on the last day, when they finished 155 behind with four wickets left.

Australia won back the Ashes with a huge 562-run victory in the final Test at the Oval, where Ponsford and Bradman broke their new record with a stand of 451 for the second wicket, still the largest stand between the countries. Bradman made 244 on the first day and played a magnificent innings, Ponsford, less certain, went on to 266. Australia made 701, and despite another century by Leyland, the match was over in four days, in which 1494 runs were scored.

1936-37
Australia 3
England 2

In the first Test of the 1936–37 series England scored 358 (Leyland 126) and 256. Australia replied with 234 (Fingleton 100) and were then caught on a rain-damaged pitch and put out for 58, England winning by 322. Voce took ten wickets and G. O. Allen, the captain, eight.

A long innings by Hammond of 231 not out enabled England to score 426 for 6 declared in the second Test, and Australia again had to bat on a wet wicket and were dismissed for 80. England won by an innings and 22.

Rain affected the play again in the third Test, this time to Australia's advantage. Bradman declared at 200 for 9 to catch England on a bad wicket. Allen declared at 76 for 9, but bad light saved Australia that day, and next day the tail enders were sent in first till the wicket eased. Fingleton (136) and Bradman (270), coming in at six and seven, then made a record Test partnership for the sixth wicket of 346, enabling Australia to win by 365 runs, despite another century by Leyland.

England led in the fourth Test on first innings by 52 (Barnett 129) but Bradman then made 212 and England failed by 148 to score the 392 required. Fleetwood-Smith took ten wickets in the match. The side winning the toss and batting first had won each match. With all to play for at Melbourne Bradman won the toss and in perfect conditions Australia scored 604 (Bradman 169, McCabe 112, Badcock 118). Heavy rain half-way through England's innings ruined any chance of saving the series and Australia won by an innings and 200.

55
'The Don' sweeps to leg in 1938.

56
Leslie Ames, who was followed by Godfrey Evans and Alan Knott in the Kent and England sides.

57
Walter Hammond, 'England's counter to Bradman', who holds the record aggregate for a rubber in Australia (905).

58
Hedley Verity, whose eight dismissals of Bradman in Tests is the highest of any bowler.

36

1938
England 1
Australia 1

Two of England's greatest batsmen, Len Hutton and Denis Compton, made their first appearances against Australia in the first Test at Trent Bridge and each scored a century. With Barnett also making a century (he reached it with the first ball after lunch on the first day) and Paynter scoring 216 not out, England declared at 658 for 8. But McCabe rescued Australia with a brilliant 232 (he made 127 of the last 148) in an innings of 411, and Bill Brown (133) and Bradman (144 not out) defended well in the follow-on to save the game.

More double centuries came in the second Test from Hammond (240) and Brown, who carried his bat for 206. Behind on the first innings, Australia again saved the game through Bradman (102 not out).

Because the Old Trafford Test was washed out, Australia's win in a low-scoring game at Leeds ensured they retained the Ashes. Bradman scored the only century, his 103 enabling Australia to score 242 and lead on first innings by 19 runs. After an opening stand of 60, England were dismissed in the second innings for 123. Bill O'Reilly took five wickets in each innings. Conditions were very poor, and Australia did not find it easy to score the 105 necessary to win. The decisive point came when Lindsay Hassett was dropped second ball. He went on to score an aggressive 33 and Australia were home by five wickets.

The fourth Test at the Oval was to be played to a finish. Both sets

59
Maurice Leyland scored seven centuries against Australia.

60
The England team at the Oval, 1938.
Back row: W. J. Edrich, sub, W. E. Bowes, L. Hutton, J. Hardstaff, D. C. S. Compton, A. Wood. *Seated:* H. Verity, K Farnes, W. R. Hammond, M. Leyland, E. Paynter.

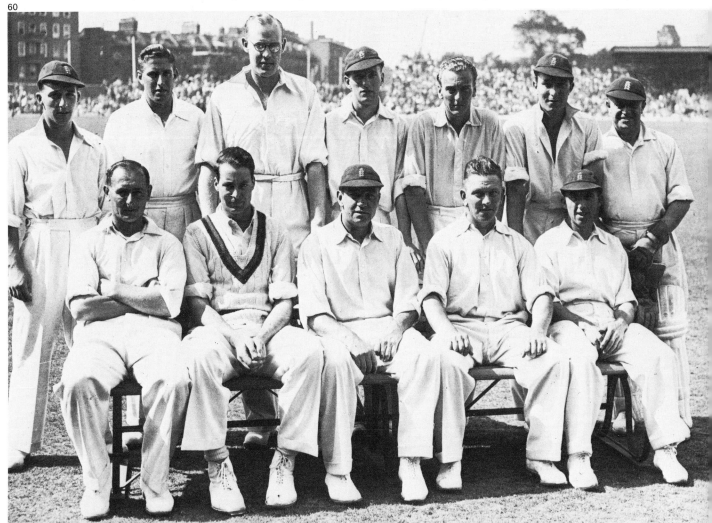

of selectors packed the sides with batting, and England were lucky enough to win the toss on a perfect wicket. The rest is cricket history. Hutton played what was then the highest and longest Test match innings (364 in 13 hours 20 minutes). He was supported by Leyland (187) and Hardstaff (169 not out) and England reached the highest Test match score of 903 for 7 declared. Fleetwood-Smith was said to have not bowled badly for 1 for 298. During this mammoth innings Bradman and Fingleton had been hurt, and without them Australia had no chance of saving the game and lost on the fourth day by an innings and 579 runs.

61
The famous groundsman 'Bosser' Martin with his roller before the scoreboard showing the final England score at the Oval, 1938.

62
The Australian tourists, 1938. *Back row:* E. L. McCormick, M. G. Waite, L. O'B. Fleetwood-Smith, W. J. O'Reilly, E. S. White, F. A. Ward, W. A. Brown, J. H. Fingleton. *Middle row:* S. G. Barnes, S. J. McCabe, D. G. Bradman, B. A. Barnett, C. W. Walker. *Front row:* A. L. Hassett, C. L. Badcock.

63

The page from Herbert Strudwick's score-book showing Len Hutton's record 364 at the Oval in 1938.

64

Hutton cuts watched by Barnett and Fingleton on his way to his record score.

63

MATCH BETWEEN	England					♂		Australia			
PLAYED AT	Kennington Oval				ON	Aug 20				1938	
UMPIRES	Messrs Chester & Walden			SIDE WINNING TOSS	England						
SCORERS	Strudwick		England 1st	INNINGS							

ORDER	TIME IN / OUT	BATSMEN	RUNS AS SCORED	HOW OUT	BOWLER	Totals
1		Hutton		ct Hassett	O'Reilly	364
2		Edrich		L. B. W	O'Reilly	12
3		Leyland		run	Out	187
4		W.R.Hammond		L. B. W	J. Smith	59
5		Paynter		L. B. W	O'Reilly	0
6		Compton		Bowled	Waite	1
7		Hardstaff		not	out	169
8		Wood		c & b	Barnes	53
9		Verity		not	out	8
10		K. Farnes	did not bat. Innings declared closed 4.30 3rd day 7 wkts			
11		Bowes				

BYES	LEG BYES	WIDES	NO BALLS	TOTAL EXTRAS	50
		Hutton 200 in 468 min		TOTAL	903

Hutton missed at score 40
50 in 75 min. 100 in 171 min. 200 in 340 min. 402 in 420 min. 451 in 470 min. &

RUNS AT THE FALL OF EACH WICKET	1 FOR 29	2 FOR 411	3 FOR 546	4 FOR 547	5 FOR 555	6 FOR 770	7 FOR 876	8 FOR	9 FOR	10 FOR

THE STRUDWICK SCORE BOOK. Copyright by H. STRUDWICK. Surrey County Cricket Club.

Printed by Wightman & Co., Ltd., Dugdale Street, S.E. 5.

64

1946-47
Australia 3
England 0

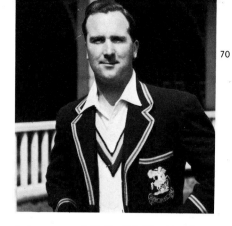

Test cricket between Australia and England resumed on November 29, 1946 at Brisbane. The war had cut short the lives of many cricketers, including some who had performed great deeds. Other careers could not span the lost years. The greatest Australian and Englishman of the 1930s, Bradman and Hammond, resumed the contest as captains, with opposite fortunes, alongside new players. Keith Miller and Godfrey Evans had already promised greatness in a series of unofficial 'Victory' Tests in England. Others making their debuts in England–Australia games included Arthur Morris, Ray Lindwall, Don Tallon, Cyril Washbrook and Alec Bedser.

The last Test before the war had seen England's biggest victory, the first afterwards provided Australia's. Australia scored 645 (Bradman 187, Hassett 128) and dismissed England for 141 (Miller 7 for 60) and 172 (Toshack 6 for 82). Bradman had had a back operation in 1946, and many doubted his ability to succeed at 38 years old. When he had scored 28 at Brisbane, he was apparently caught by Ikin off Voce. Bradman has said since that he played the ball into the ground, and the umpire agreed. It was a decision which had continuing influence, for Bradman, who must have considered retirement before the series, made over 1000 more runs against England, and delighted followers in both countries.

Australia made another huge score in the second Test at Sydney, 659 for 8 declared, and again won by an innings, despite a gallant 119 by Bill Edrich. Sid Barnes and Bradman each made 234, and Ian

Johnson and Colin McCool each took eight wickets. The third and fourth Tests were drawn. In the former, Lindwall and McCool made their only centuries against England, and in the latter Arthur Morris and Denis Compton both scored a century in each innings. Australia won the fifth Test at Sydney by five wickets, Lindwall getting his best analysis so far in the first innings, 7 for 63. Doug Wright also took seven wickets in Australia's first innings.

Len Hutton, who now had a shortened left arm after a war-time accident in a gymnasium, showed remarkable determination to regain his eminence, his last three innings in the series being 94, 76 and 122 not out. Hammond, sadly, failed, and after averaging only 21 in the first four Tests, he was left out of the side for the last Test and did not play against Australia again. The Tests were watched by 850,000 spectators, proving big cricket to be as popular as ever.

70
England's acrobatic wicketkeeper in 31 Tests against Australia, Godfrey Evans.

65–69
The England touring party of 1946–47. *from the top, left to right:* N. W. D. Yardley, T. G. Evans, T. P. B. Smith, L. Hutton, A. V. Bedser, J. Hardstaff, W. Voce, R. Pollard, W. R. Hammond, J. T. Ikin, W. J. Edrich, James Langridge, P. Gibb, Major Howard (manager), L. B. Fishlock, C. Washbrook, D. V. P. Wright, D. C. S. Compton.

65–69

71
England's best post-war opening pair, Len Hutton and Cyril Washbrook.

72
Australia's opening batsmen in the immediate post-war years, Arthur Morris and Sid Barnes.

73
Former Test cricketers at Adelaide for the fourth Test in 1947, where they were reporting on the game. *Back row:* W. A. Oldfield, (Australia), S. J. McCabe (A), A. F. Kippax (A), W. E. Bowes (England), W. J. O'Reilly (A), H. L. Hendry (A), C. V. Grimmett (A), A. Richardson (A), G. Duckworth (E). *Middle row:* V. Y. Richardson (A), A. E. R. Gilligan (E), W. M. Woodfull (A), W. W. Armstrong (A), H. L. Collins (A), H. Ironmonger (A), A. A. Mailey (A). *Front row:* L. Darling (A), J. H. Fingleton (A).

71

72

73

1948 England 0 Australia 4

With Bill Johnston and Neil Harvey making their debuts against England in 1948, to play alongside Morris, Hassett, Bradman, Barnes, Miller, Johnson, Tallon and Toshack, the Australian sides of that year can claim to be the best ever. England were lucky that Denis Compton was at his best to equal some great performances by the Australians.

Australia won the first Test by

74
D. V. P. Wright's unusual leg-break action is well shown by this picture.

75
Denis Compton breaking his wicket as he fell after making 184 at Trent Bridge in the first Test, 1948.

eight wickets with Bradman and Hassett scoring centuries and Bill Johnston taking nine wickets. Compton scored 184 for England, and Laker got four wickets in his first Test against Australia. Australia won the second Test by 409 runs, Morris and Barnes scoring centuries.

England had the better of the third Test, drawn when the fourth day was washed out. Hutton, to everybody's astonishment, had been dropped after apparently being unsettled by bumpers. Compton arrived at the wicket on the first day with the score 28 for 2, to be greeted by a series of bumpers from Lindwall. Four runs later he had edged a no-ball onto his forehead and was led from the field with blood pouring from his head. Compton had his forehead stitched, and it was announced that he would bat if needed. At 119 for 5, he *was* needed. Compton then played one of cricket's memorable innings, scoring 145 not out and giving England a first-innings lead of 142.

Hutton was back for the fourth Test at Leeds. With 81 from him, 143 from Washbrook, 111 from Edrich and 79 from night watch-man Bedser, England reached 423

before the third wicket fell. How could they lose? But Harvey made a century on his debut against England, and England's declaration after five minutes on the last day left Australia to get 404 to win in 345 minutes. With Morris getting 182 and Bradman 173 not out, Australia scored 404 for 3, and won with fifteen minutes to spare.

It was the Australian bowlers' turn at the Oval in the fifth Test, although Morris scored 196. England were dismissed for 52, Lindwall, at his fastest and best, taking 6 for 20. Hutton alone played him with confidence, being last out for 30. Bradman was clapped all the way to the wicket for his last Test innings and given three cheers by the England players. It was an emotional moment, too much, perhaps, for his concentration. Needing four for a Test match average of 100, he was bowled second ball by Eric Hollies for a duck, and was clapped all the way back. Nevertheless, Australia won by an innings.

42

76

76
Arthur Morris run out by Evans when four short of a double century in the fifth Test at the Oval, 1948.

77

77
The Australian tourists of 1948. *Back row:* R. Lindwall, K. Miller, W. Brown. *Middle row:* W. Ferguson (scorer), N. Harvey, D. Ring, E. Toshack, W. Johnston, R. Saggers, S. Barnes, G. Johnson (manager). *Front row:* S. Loxton, R. Hamence, L. Hassett, D. Bradman (captain), C. McCool, A. Morris, I. Johnson.

78
The England team being presented to the Duke of Edinburgh, who is seen shaking hands with Bedser. Others seen in the picture are *from right* Laker, Bailey, Compton, Evans.

79
A conclusive run out in the second Test at Melbourne, 1950 with Harvey the victim.

80
England's youngest-ever Test player, Brian Close, out lbw to Johnston in the second Test, 1950.

78

79

1950-51
Australia 4
England 1

England introduced some new players to England–Australia matches on the tour of 1950–51, principally Trevor Bailey and Reg Simpson. Apart from Jack Iverson, a spinner who topped the averages, Australia relied mainly on the old guard and confirmed their superiority.

Rain produced some freak scores in the first Test at Brisbane. England did well to dismiss Australia for 228 on the first day. A downpour next day meant that when England batted on Monday, and the sun came out, a real sticky wicket developed. England went from 49 for 1 to 68 for 7, when they declared. Australia also declared at 32 for 7, and England were 30 for 6 at the close. Nineteen wickets had fallen for 81 runs. The wicket was easier next day, but although Hutton reached 62 not out, England failed by 70 to reach their target.

The luck stayed with Australia throughout the series. The second Test was won by 28 runs, the third more easily by an innings and thirteen, thanks to 145 not out by Miller. Arthur Morris scored 206 in the fourth Test, and Hutton carried his bat for 156 not out. J. W. Burke made his only century against England on his Test debut. England at last won the fifth Test by 8 wickets, thanks to 156 not out by Simpson, 79 and 60 not out by Hutton, and five wickets in each innings by Alec Bedser.

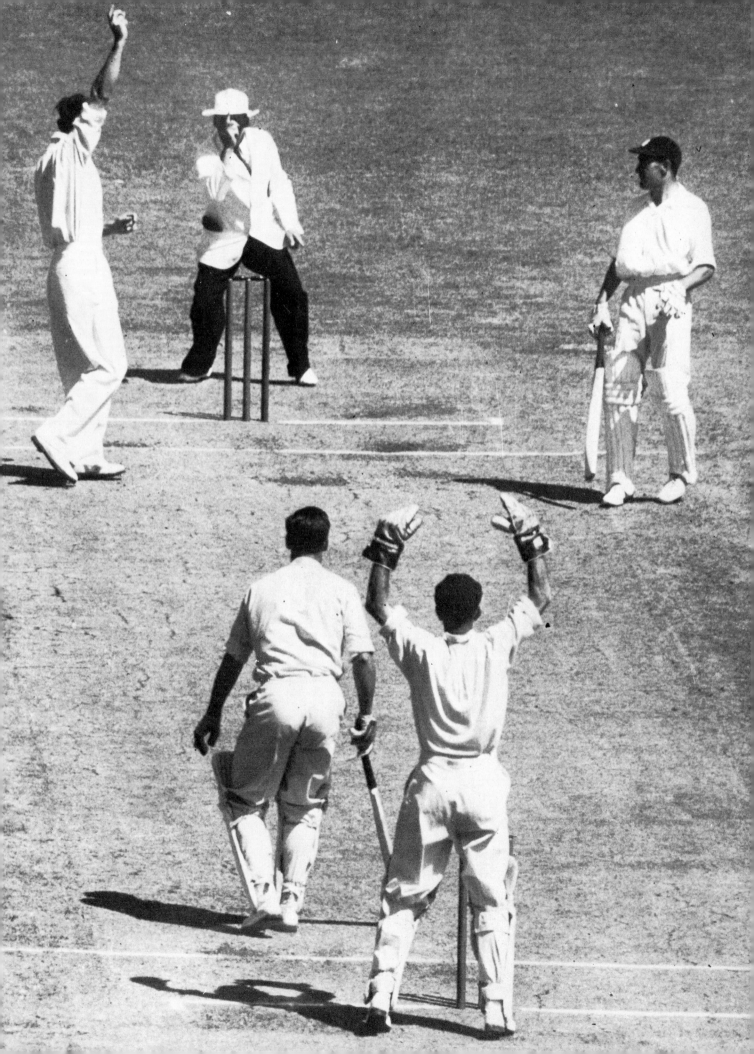

1953
England 1
Australia 0

Because of rain, there were more draws in the 1953 series than in the three previous series together. Four English giants, Peter May, Brian Statham, Tom Graveney and Fred Trueman made their first appearances against Australia and Aussie greats Richie Benaud and Alan Davidson played their first game against England.

The first Test was spoiled by rain after Hassett had made a century and Bedser taken fourteen wickets. The second Test at Lord's was an exciting draw, notable for the fine defensive innings of Willie Watson. Australia made 346 (Hassett 104) and England replied with 372 (Hutton 145). In their

81
Going out to bat, Sheppard and Don Kenyon, who was to become an England selector.

82
The valiant efforts of Lindwall were not enough to save the Ashes in the fifth Test at the Oval, 1953. Graveney is the batsman.

83
Four England captains after inspecting the wicket during the third Test of 1953 at Old Trafford: N. W. D. Yardley, Sir Len Hutton, R. E. S. Wyatt, F. R. Brown.

THE MEN WHO WON THE ASHES

Your special souvenir picture

THE ASHES

Tock with the up, run up
and Tylecote return
win will ring loud,
crowd will feel proud
and Bates with the sun,
home with the...

BACK ROW
(left to right)

Trevor Bailey — Back-to-the-wall hero of the Tests. He is 30, and this season must rank as one of the world's best all-rounders. Scored 222 runs in all five games, took eight wickets for an average of 48. Played in 19 Tests. Lives at Westcliff, Essex.

P. B. H. May — Not yet 24 but already almost a veteran. Dropped after the first Test and recalled for the last. He is a stockbroker and, like Bailey, a Cambridge Blue. Played in eight Tests.

T. W. Graveney — Aged 26, born Northumberland. Played in all five Tests (average 24.14) with a highest of 78. Made county debut in 1948 and played in 14 Tests. Scored 175 against India at Bombay in 1951.

J. Laker — Off-break bowler who, with Surrey colleague Lock, changed Oval's dust into England's Ashes, aged 31, and Bradford born. Played in last three Tests and took nine wickets for an average of 23.55. Played in 18 Tests.

J. Wardle — The chirpy chappie from Yorkshire. His slow left-arm bowling captured 13 wickets (average 26.46) in second and third Tests, and scored a total of 57 runs. He is 30 and was born at Ardsley, Yorks.

Tony Lock — England's other "victory" bowler—slow left-arm. Aged 23 and was born at Limpsfield. Injury to spinning finger kept him out of first three Tests. In last two he took eight wickets at a cost of 20.62 each. His share in the Australian collapse at the Oval was five for 45.

F. S. Trueman — The Yorkshire thunderbolt who "appeared" on the cricket scene last season when he routed the Indian touring team at Old Trafford. A loss of form put a query mark after his name right up to the last Test against the Australians when he took four wickets for 90. Formerly a miner, now 22, he is doing National Service.

FRONT ROW
(left to right)

W. J. Edrich — One of the Norfolk cricketing family. Hutton's opening partner in last three Tests and made a total of 156 runs. Highest score: the 64 he scored at Leeds in the fourth Test. Aged 37. Played in 34 Tests.

Alec Bedser — One of Surrey's famous twins. Born at Reading, 1918, currently the world's greatest right-hand fast-medium bowler. Played in all five Tests, took 39 wickets for an average of 17.48 and smashed the world record (38) for the most wickets in an England-Australian series previously held by Maurice Tate. Twice took seven Australian wickets in an innings in the series just over. Played in 47 Tests.

Len Hutton — First professional to skipper England against Australia and will lead England in the West Indies. Made more runs (443) than any man on either side in the Test series just ended, and made top score, 145, finishing with the highest average—55.37. Born Pudsey, Yorks, is 37 and has played in 65 Tests and holds Test record innings of 364 against Australia.

Denis Compton — The "Golden Boy of Lord's." Born at Hendon, is 35, and an unorthodox right-hand bat and slow left-arm bowler. Played in all five Tests and scored 234 runs. Has played in 54 Tests since 1946. In 1947 scored over 1,000 runs and dismissed 93 batsmen. Made his county debut in 1939. Free-hitting batsman and brilliant runner between wickets. Scored 117 runs in Test series just ended (average 23). Played in 49 Tests. Highest score this series was 61 at Leeds.

Godfrey Evans — Acknowledged to be the finest wicket-keeper in the world.

The men in white coats in back row are (extreme left) Umpire Dai Davies; (centre) Stanley Tait, masseur; and (extreme right) Umpire Frank Lee.

Here are the men who brought the Ashes back to England after 20 years.

---

second knock, Australia made 368 and at the close of the fourth day England had lost Hutton, Don Kenyon and Graveney for 20. Watson had also given a half-chance. On the last day Watson (109), ably assisted by Bailey (71) took England to 282 for 7 and saved the day against Lindwall, Johnston *et al.*

Rain spoiled the third Test, in which 122 from Neil Harvey gave Australia a first-innings lead of 42, but Australia, batting again, were 35 for 8 at the close. The Australians were not happy with Bailey's bowling in the fourth Test. Largely through Bailey's batting (4 hours 10 minutes for 38), Australia were left to get 177 to win in 115 minutes. They made a good try, but Bailey, taking his time, bowled six overs down the leg side for nine runs. Australia finished 30 short.

England regained the Ashes in the fifth Test at the Oval. Getting a first-innings lead of 31, England

84
Neil Harvey driving a ball from Wardle during his 122 in the third Test in 1953.

85
Bill Edrich is caught by Hole in the third Test, 1953. Others pictured are *from left:* Hassett, Langley, Lindwall, Hutton and Davidson.

86
A contemporary newspaper acclaims England's first post-war Ashes success. *Back row:* D. Davies (umpire), T. Bailey, P. May, T. Graveney, S. Tait (masseur), J. Laker, G. A. R. Lock, J. Wardle, F. Trueman, F. Lee (umpire). *Front row:* W. J. Edrich, A. Bedser, L. Hutton (captain), D. Compton, T. G. Evans.

87
Hero of England's rearguard action in the second Test, Willie Watson.

dismissed Australia for 162, and knocked off the runs for two wickets. Stalwarts Edrich and Compton were batting when the winning runs came. It was like 1926, a lone win at the Oval breaking Australian post-war domination. Alec Bedser was the man of the series, taking 39 wickets, then a record for an England–Australia rubber.

87

1954-55
Australia 1
England 3

Australia scored 601 for 8 declared in the first Test, in which Colin Cowdrey made his Test debut. Bedser took 1 for 131, and, despite his record the previous year, did not play against Australia again. In the light of the rest of the tour, it is remarkable that Frank Tyson, playing against Australia for the first time, took 1 for 160. Morris scored 153, Harvey 162 and Australia won by an innings and 154. Nevertheless Len Hutton decided that pure speed from Tyson and Statham would prove Australia's undoing. In the second Test Australia obtained a first-

innings lead of 74, but May scored a century and Australia were set 223 to win. Despite 92 not out from Harvey, Australia were dismissed for 184, Tyson 6 for 85. The supremacy of Tyson was established, and in the third Test Australia, set to score 240 to win, were out for 111, Tyson 7 for 27. Cowdry scored 102, and Australia again lost after leading on the first innings. Australia batted first in the fourth Test, but were again out for 111 in the second innings, leaving England only 94 to get to win, which were obtained for the loss of five wickets.

The fifth Test was spoiled by rain, but with Graveney this time scoring a century. Australia followed on and were still 32 behind with only 4 wickets left at the close. Tyson took 28 wickets in the series and Statham 18, and Australia had no answer to their pace.

1956 England 2 Australia 1

Len Hutton retired after his successful captaincy in Australia, and Peter May took over to lead England against Ian Johnson's tourists.

Rain spoiled the first Test, and Australia won the second at Lord's by 185 runs, thanks to some marvellous bowling by Miller, who took five wickets in each innings, and to a record nine dismissals by wicket-keeper Gil Langley. England levelled the score in the third Test, winning by an innings and 43 runs. May scored 101, Laker took eleven wickets and Lock seven. Cyril Washbrook was recalled to the England side, and scored 98, helping May take the score from 17 for 3 (Ron Archer took all three) to 204 for 4.

The fourth Test was one of the most remarkable of all time. The Reverend David Sheppard was recalled to the England side and scored 113. Peter Richardson made 104 and England totalled 459. Tony Lock took the first Australian wicket to fall at 48, at which time Jim Laker had 0 for 21. In the next 7·4 overs he took 9 for 16, and at the close of the second day he had 1 for 17 in the follow-on. Rain prevented much play on

88
Frank Tyson bowling in the fourth Test at Adelaide, 1955. Colin McDonald is the non-striking batsman.

89
Colin Cowdrey in his early Kent days.

90
Frank Tyson, destroyer of Australia in 1954–55.

91
David Sheppard batting against Australia at the Oval in 1956. Maddocks is keeping wicket.

the third and fourth days, one
more Australian wicket falling to
Laker. On the final day Laker took
the remaining eight. Colin
McDonald played a gallant innings
of 89. Laker's figures were 9 for 37
and 10 for 53, a record 19 wickets
for any form of cricket. It is
inexplicable that Lock, bowling
more overs than Laker, took only
one wicket at the other end.

  More rain at the Oval deprived
Australia of any chance to level the
series, and Laker took seven more
wickets to finish with 46 at an
average of 9·60. Surprisingly this
is not an overall Test record, Syd
Barnes having taken 49 South
African wickets in 1913–14.

92
Jim Laker in action.

93
In each of his eight Test innings in 1956,
Peter Richardson was caught by the
wicket-keeper.

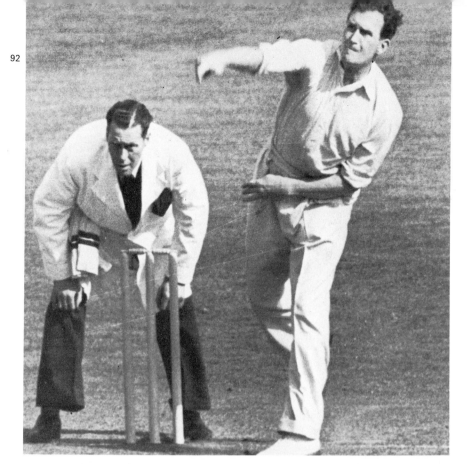
92

93

94
For Surrey and England Tony Lock bowled
many overs at the other end from Laker.
Emigrating later, he became a successful
captain of Western Australia.

95
The scorecard of 'Laker's match' tells its
own tale.

94

95 ENGLAND

P. E. Richardson	c Maddocks b Benaud	104
M. C. Cowdrey	c Maddocks b Lindwall	80
Rev. D. S. Sheppard	b Archer	113
P. B. H. May	c Archer b Benaud	43
T. E. Bailey	b Johnson	20
C. Washbrook	lbw Johnson	6
A. S. M. Oakman	c Archer b Johnson	10
T. G. Evans	st Maddocks b Johnson	47
J. C. Laker	run out	3
G. A. R. Lock	not out	25
J. B. Statham	c Maddocks b Lindwall	0
Extras	(b 2, lb 5, w 1)	8
Total		**459**

AUSTRALIA

C. C. McDonald	c Lock b Laker	32	c Oakman b Laker	89
J. W. Burke	c Cowdrey b Lock	22	c Lock b Laker	33
R. N. Harvey	b Laker	0	c Cowdrey b Laker	0
I. D. Craig	lbw Laker	8	lbw Laker	38
K. R. Miller	c Oakman b Laker	6	b Laker	0
K. D. Mackay	c Oakman b Laker	0	c Oakman b Laker	0
R. G. Archer	st Evans b Laker	6	c Oakman b Laker	0
R. Benaud	c Statham b Laker	0	b Laker	18
R. R. Lindwall	not out	6	c Lock b Laker	8
L. V. Maddocks	b Laker	4	lbw Laker	2
I. W. Johnson	b Laker	0	not out	1
Extras		0	(b 12, lb 4)	16
Total		**84**	**Total**	**205**

FALL OF WICKETS
ENGLAND

Wkt	1st	2nd
1st	174	—
2nd	195	—
3rd	288	—
4th	321	—
5th	327	—
6th	339	—
7th	401	—
8th	417	—
9th	458	—
10th	459	—

AUSTRALIA

Wkt	1st	2nd
1st	48	28
2nd	48	55
3rd	62	114
4th	62	124
5th	62	130
6th	73	130
7th	73	181
8th	78	198
9th	84	203
10th	84	205

UMPIRES:
F. S. LEE,
E. DAVIS

AUSTRALIA 1st Innings

	O	M	R	W
Lindwall	21·3	6	63	2
Miller	21	6	41	0
Archer	22	6	73	1
Johnson	47	10	151	4
Benaud	47	17	123	2

ENGLAND

	1st Innings				2nd Innings			
	O	M	R	W	O	M	R	W
Statham	6	3	6	0	16	10	15	0
Bailey	4	3	4	0	20	8	31	0
Laker	16·4	4	37	9	51·2	23	53	10
Lock	14	3	37	1	55	30	69	0
Oakman					8	3	21	0

96

96
The Australian tourists of 1956. *Back row:* J. Wilson, K. Mackay, A. Davidson, P. Burge, P. Crawford, R. Benaud, R. Archer, N. Harvey. *Middle row:* G. Langley, K. Miller, I. Johnson (captain), R. Lindwall, C. McDonald, J. Burke. *Front row:* I. Craig, L. Maddocks, J. Rutherford.

1958-59
Australia 4
England 0

Richie Benaud captained Australia in the 1958–59 series. Norman O'Neill made his debut for Australia in the first test, and settled a low-scoring match by scoring 71 not out in the second innings, Australia winning by eight wickets. In the second Test May scored 113 and Harvey countered with 167. Statham took seven wickets and Davidson six in the first innings. England collapsed to Ian Meckiff (6 for 38) in the second innings, being all out 87, and Australia won by eight wickets again.

In the third Test May (92) and Cowdrey (100 not out) put on 182 in England's second innings and saved the match against some fine bowling by Benaud, who took nine wickets. Colin McDonald made 170 in the fourth Test, and Australia won again, this time by ten wickets. Another century by McDonald, this time 133, led to a nine-wicket win for Australia in the final Test.

There was controversy over the bowling actions of some Australian bowlers in this series. England began with what was thought to be the strongest Test side in the world, but the rout by Meckiff in the second Test seemed to dishearten them. Many Englishmen thought that Meckiff threw, and there were also doubts about Slater and Rorke, with his great drag. None of them played against England again.

However Davidson took most wickets, and he and Benaud proved themselves real world class. O'Neill and McDonald batted excellently, and Australia generally showed more urgency and enthusiasm than England.

97
One of Australia's best baseball players, Norman O'Neill was a hard-hitting batsman and brilliant fielder.

98
The stylish left-hander Neil Harvey, who has scored more runs than any other Australian in post-war Tests.

99
McDonald and Mackay resuming Australia's first innings in the final Test at Melbourne, 1958–59. McDonald's 133 enabled Australia to win convincingly.

100
100
A classic cover drive by England captain, Peter May.

101
The 23-year-old Ted Dexter arriving in Australia to join the 1958–59 touring party.

102
Davidson failed to hold this chance offered in the 1958–59 Brisbane Test by Graveney off Benaud, anxiously watched by wicket-keeper Grout.

101

102

104

103
The Australian tourists of 1961. *Back row:* B. Booth, W. Lawry, F. Misson, R. Gaunt, G. McKenzie. *Middle row:* A. James (physiotherapist), J. Cameron (scorer), B. Jarman, I. Quick, R. Steele (treasurer), L. Kline, N. O'Neill, P. Burge, R. Simpson. *Front row:* W. Grout, A. Davidson, R. Benaud (captain), S. G. Webb (manager), N. Harvey, C. McDonald, K. Mackay.

104
Brian Close, who was only 19 when selected for the tour of Australia in 1950.

105
Bill Lawry first toured England in 1961 and shares the first wicket record partnership for Australia against England, putting on 244 runs with Bobby Simpson at Adelaide in the 1965–66 series.

106
Richie Benaud bowling in his greatest match. He took 6 for 70 at Old Trafford in 1961 to retain the Ashes for Australia.

107
Norman O'Neill on his way to his first Test century against England at the Oval, 1961.

Benaud's first Test side in England included newcomer Bill Lawry, and Graham McKenzie made his debut in the second Test. England had several men playing against Australia for the first time, principally Ken Barrington, Mike Smith and Ray Illingworth.

In the first Test Australia led on the first innings by 321, Harvey getting 114, but 112 from Subba Row and 180 from Dexter saw England comfortably save the game at 401 for four. Australia won the second Test by five wickets with the help of 130 from Lawry and eight catches by wicket-keeper Wally Grout. England levelled by winning the third Test by eight wickets, Fred Trueman taking eleven wickets on his home ground at Leeds.

The fourth Test was one of the great matches, and it won the series for Australia. Australia were dismissed for 190, Statham getting five wickets, and England replied with 367 (May 95, Barrington 78, Pullar 63). In their second knock, Australia were 334 for 9, only 157 ahead, and seemed doomed. The last day saw some remarkable cricket. In the morning Davidson (77 not out) and McKenzie (32) added 92 for the last wicket, raising England's target to 256 at more than one a minute. Dexter slashed the Australians for 76, and at 150 for one England seemed home. Benaud then went round the wicket to pitch his leg-breaks in the rough caused by the bowlers' footmarks. Dexter was caught behind, and May bowled round his legs for a duck. England collapsed and Australia won by 54, Benaud 6 for 70. The final Test was drawn, Subba Row, O'Neill and Burge getting centuries.

1962-63
Australia 1
England 1

Dexter led England in Australia in 1962–63. A high-scoring first Test was drawn, all the batsmen getting a few, Brian Booth the most with 112. Booth scored another century in the second Test, but it could not save Australia from a seven-wicket defeat, Cowdrey and David Sheppard each getting 113. Australia came back with an eight-wicket win in the next Test, Davidson bowling beautifully for nine wickets.

Batsmen were generally on top in this series and the last two Tests were drawn, Australia retaining the Ashes. Barrington scored 582 runs, and Davidson was the most successful bowler with 24 wickets. The run rate was generally slow, thus depriving large crowds of some potentially exciting finishes.

110

108
Brian Statham, who bowled in six series
against Australia, from 1953 to 1962.

109
England's captain in 1962–63 and 1964,
Ted Dexter played many dashing innings.

110
Alan Davidson bowls Geoff Pullar for 11
in the second Test at Melbourne, 1962–63.

111
Bobby Simpson drives in the fourth Test
match at Adelaide, 1962–63, on his way
to 71 in the second innings.

112
The first Test of the 1962–63 series.
O'Neill swings at and misses a no-ball
from Fred Trueman.

111

112

1964
England 0
Australia 1

Rain spoiled the 1964 series, in which Geoff Boycott, John Edrich and Derek Underwood played their first games against Australia and Ian Redpath made his debut against England. England led on first innings in the first two Tests, both drawn, John Edrich scoring 120 on his first meeting with Australian bowlers. The third Test decided the series, and Peter Burge won it. England scored 268, and seemed to be heading for another first-innings lead with Australia 178 for seven. Dexter then took the new ball, a decision which perhaps lost the series. Burge played a great innings, scoring 160, and adding 105 with Neil Hawke (37) and 89 with Wally Grout (37). Australia led by 121 and won by seven wickets. The fourth Test was for statisticians only. Lawry and captain Bobby Simpson scored 201 for the first wicket, and Simpson went on to score 311 in a total of 656 for 8 declared. Dexter (174) and Barrington (256) then added 246 for England's third wicket. England scored 611, and only two overs were bowled in Australia's second innings.

113
Only Bradman and Sutcliffe of players who have made over 2000 runs in England—Australia Tests have a better average than Ken Barrington.

114
Peter Burge's great innings of 160 won the game and the Ashes for Australia in the third Test of 1964.

115
This shot by Dexter off McKenzie lost him his wicket, caught O'Neill for 68, in the first Test of 1964.

The last day of the fifth Test was lost through rain, but Boycott made his first century against Australia, and when Fred Trueman had Neil Hawke caught by Cowdrey in the slips he became the first cricketer to take 300 Test wickets.

116
Fred Trueman, whose record of 307 Test wickets was overhauled by Lance Gibbs in 1976.

117
The Australia touring party of 1964. *Back row:* D. Sherwood (scorer), R. Cowper, R. Sellers, I. Redpath, J. Potter, T. Veivers, A. James (scorer). *Middle row:* N. Hawke, W. Lawry, G. McKenzie, J. Ledward (treasurer), A. Connolly, G. Corling, J. Martin. *Front row:* A. Grout, P. Burge, R. Simpson (captain), R. Steele (manager), B. Booth, N. O'Neill, B. Jarman.

117

1965-66
Australia 1
England 1

Although Bill Lawry scored 166 in the first Test match, most attention centred on Doug Walters, who scored 155 in his first Test. Australia had the better of a rain-affected draw. Fifteen players bowled in the second Test, where Walters scored another century. Burge, John Edrich and Cowdrey also reached three figures. England could not capitalize on a first-innings lead of 200, but won the third Test after a magnificent 185 by Bob Barber, who with Boycott (84) and Edrich (103) took England past 300 with one wicket down. England won by an innings and 93. Not for the first time, Australia levelled the score in the next Test, winning by an innings and nine runs. Batting second, Lawry (119) and Simpson (225) decided to break up the England fielding by taking quick singles. They were so successful that 93 singles came in Australia's record opening partnership of 244. Despite a century from Barrington, Australia won easily, and their captain, Simpson, one of the greatest-ever slip fielders, described the catch by wicket-keeper Wally Grout to dismiss Cowdrey as the best he'd seen. In this match, Ian Chappell and Keith Stackpole, batting at seven and eight, made their debuts against England. Barrington and Lawry each scored further centuries in the fifth Test (Lawry's third of the series) but Bob Cowper took the batting honours with 307 in a match which always looked a draw.

118

119

118
Alan Connolly made his debut against England in the 1965–66 series, but bowled best in England in 1968.

119
Graham McKenzie bowled in six series against England from 1961 to 1970.

120
Bob Barber's best innings for England was 185 in the third Test of the 1965–66 series.

121
The England tourists of 1965–66. *Back row:* J. Ikin (assistant manager), D. J. Brown, L. D. Larter, K. Higgs, J. Jennings (masseur). *Middle row:* P. H. Parfitt, G. Boycott, W. E. Russell, R. W. Barber, I. J. Jones, B. Knight, J. H. Edrich. *Front row:* J. M. Parks, F. J. Titmus, M. C. Cowdrey, M. J. K. Smith (captain), S. C. Griffith (manager), K. F. Barrington, D. A. Allen, J. T. Murray.

120

121

122
Tom Graveney's elegant batting was seen on three tours of Australia between 1954 and 1963.

123
Neil Hawke bowled well against England in the 1960s, but some remember him as Trueman's 300th Test victim.

124
John Gleeson made his debut against England in 1968, and played in all five Tests.

124

1968
England 1
Australia 1

After his fine performances in Australia, Bill Lawry took over from Bobby Simpson as Australia's captain, and Colin Cowdrey replaced Mike Smith as England's skipper. In the first Test Dennis Amiss (with two ducks) and Basil d'Oliveira played against Australia for the first time, and John Snow, with no fewer than 60 Test wickets against all the other Test countries to his credit, finally got his first chance against the Australians.

Australia won the first Test by 159 runs, Bob Cowper doing most damage with 4 for 48 in the first innings. Rain spoiled the second Test, the two hundredth between the countries. Colin Milburn scored a great 83, but England lacked the time to force a win after dismissing Australia for 78. England were foiled by rain again in the third Test, where a century by Cowdrey gave them a first-innings lead of 117. England's frustration continued in the fourth Test, where only 96 were needed with six wickets in hand at the close. It seemed that rain would also save Australia in the last Test at the Oval. Big scores were made by Edrich (164), d'Oliveira (158) and Lawry (135), and Australia needed 352 to win in the fourth innings. Torrential rain stopped play at 4.15 when Australia had lost five wickets. Cowdrey then persuaded spectators to help clear the water, and England were left with 35 minutes to get the last five wickets. Derek Underwood claimed four of them to finish with 7 for 50, and England won by 226 runs to level a series they should have won with six minutes to spare.

125
After scoring 158 against Australia in the
final Test at the Oval in 1968, Basil
d'Oliveira was omitted from the South
African touring party. His later selection
caused the tour to be cancelled. Jarman
is the wicket keeper during his fine innings.

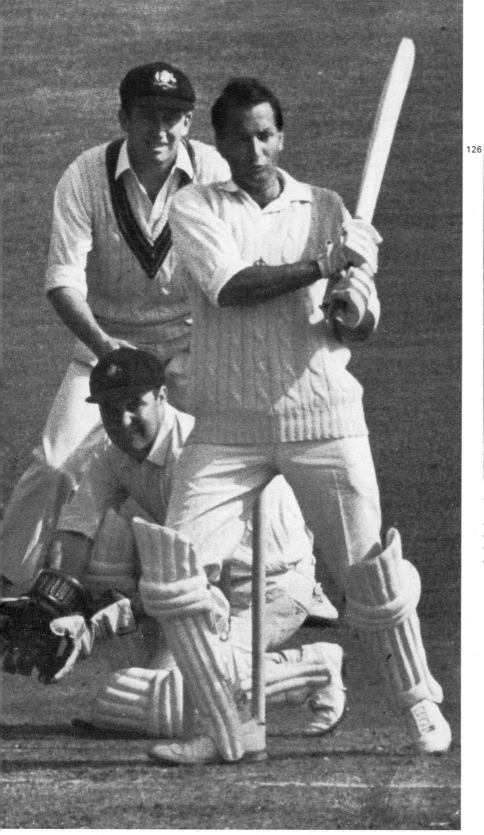

126
Colin Milburn's aggressive 83 on a difficult
wicket at Lord's in 1968 emphasizes
what a great loss he was to Test cricket
when a car injury cost him the sight of an
eye.

1970-71 Australia 0 England 2

Six Test matches were scheduled for the 1970–71 tour by England, and a seventh was added when the third Test at Melbourne was completely washed out. The series was marred by dissent between the England management and players, the anger of England players over some umpiring decisions and unpleasant crowd participation at Sydney.

In the first Test Australia passed 400 with only 3 wickets down, but were out for 433, Snow taking 6 for 114. Keith Stackpole made 207, although the English (and many Australians) thought he had been run out at 18. Walters scored 112. England secured a lead and dismissed Australia for 214, but had to accept a draw. The second Test was also drawn, with Brian Luckhurst and Edrich making centuries and Redpath (171) and Greg Chappell (108 in his first Test) putting on 219 for the sixth wicket for Australia. With no play in the third Test, England won the fourth by 299 runs. After England gained a lead of 96, Boycott scored a magnificent 142 not out in the second innings, and Australia were set 416 to win. Lawry carried his bat for 60, but Snow had 7 for 40 and Australia were out for 116.

Ian Chappell, Luckhurst and d'Oliveira scored centuries in the fifth Test, and Rodney Marsh

might have had a first Test century, too, being 92 not out when Lawry declared. Set to score 271, England were 161 for 0 at the close.

The sixth Test started sensationally when Boycott, on 58, was given run out and threw his bat down in disgust. The way to the pavilion was pointed out to him by some Australians. Edrich made 130, and Australia scored exactly half of England's 470. Dennis Lillee, in his Test debut, took 5 for 84. Illingworth did not enforce the follow on, and an unrepentant Boycott made 119 not out in the second innings. Stackpole and Ian Chappell scored centuries in reply and Australia comfortably saved the game.

127
John Snow, chief destroyer of the Australians in the 1970–71 series, gets the wicket of Bill Lawry, caught behind by Alan Knott, for 4 in the first Test at Brisbane.

128
Keith Stackpole hooks a ball from Derek Underwood to the boundary during his innings of 207 in the first Test, 1970–71.

129
Geoff Boycott, England's chief run-getter in the 1970–71 series, whose innings of 142 not out helped to win the fourth Test.

130
Ian Chappell catches Basil D'Oliveira off Dennis Lillee in the final Test, 1970–71. Dolly made 47.

Australia gave themselves a chance of saving the series in the final Test by getting a first-innings lead of 80. Lawry had been dropped, and Ian Chappell was captain for the first time. Soon after Australia went ahead a ball from Snow hit Terry Jenner on the head, sending him to hospital. Snow was warned for intimidatory bowling, a decision which angered him and captain Illingworth. At the end of the over, Snow went to field on the boundary, where he was grabbed by a spectator. Beer cans were thrown, and Illingworth took the players off the field until peace was restored. Solid batting all the way down saw England score 302 in the second innings, leaving Australia 223 to win. After bowling Eastwood for 0, Snow tore his hand on the boundary fence, and was under anaesthetic in hospital when the Ashes, which he had done much to win, were finally regained by England. Australia could muster only 160, and were beaten by 62 runs.

131

132

131
A typical hook shot by Keith Stackpole against England at Trent Bridge in 1972.

132
Ray Illingworth, captain of the Ashes-winning England side of 1970–71, bowling against the Australians in the fourth Test at Headingley in 1972.

133
Ian Chappell and Keith Stackpole join Australian keeper Rodney Marsh in a stumping appeal at Old Trafford, 1972.

134
Mike Smith, England captain on the 1965–66 tour of Australia was recalled to the side for the first Test of the 1972 series.

1972
England 2
Australia 2

England's supremacy continued in the first Test at Old Trafford. Tony Greig (57 and 63) was top scorer for England in both innings in his first match against Australia, Snow got four wickets in each innings and Lillee six in the second innings. England were on top throughout, and even a great knock of 91 by Rod Marsh could not prevent an 89-run defeat.

The Lord's Test provided one of the most amazing performances of all time, when Bob Massie, in the first of only six Tests he has played, took 8 for 84 in the first innings and 8 for 53 in the second. Greg Chappell (131) held Australia together and a lead of 36 proved more than enough when Massie skittled England for 116, Australia winning by eight wickets.

Australia had the better of the third Test, a century by Stackpole and a great 170 not out by Ross Edwards allowing them ten hours to dismiss England for under 450. However at 290 for 4 England comfortably saved the game. The Aussies were not happy about the Headingley wicket for the fourth Test, imagining it to be a 'special' for Underwood, but in fact they had the best of the wicket in the first innings and batted badly to be out for 146. At 128 for 7 England seemed to be in equal trouble, but a stand of 104 by Illingworth (57) and Snow (48) turned the game. Underwood caused havoc with 6 for 45 when Australia batted again and England required only 20 to win in the fourth innings.

Fine bowling by Lillee (5 for 58) dismissed England for 284 at the Oval, despite an aggressive 92 from Alan Knott. Ian and Greg Chappell, with a century apiece, obtained a lead of 115 for Australia,

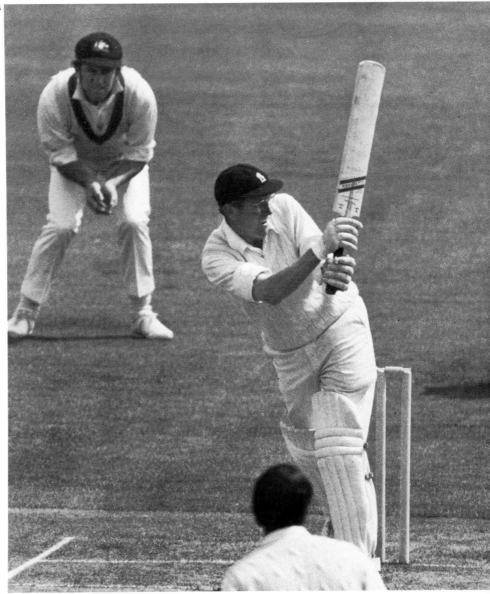

but solid batting by England
(Barry Wood getting 90 in his
first Test) allowed them to set the
Aussies a target of 242. Paul
Sheahan and Rod Marsh saw them
home with an unbeaten stand of 71
for the sixth wicket.

135
Basil D'Oliveira and Rodney Marsh in
action in the third Test at Trent Bridge,
1972.

136
John Inverarity cutting. Inverarity toured
England in 1968 and 1972.

137
Derek Underwood bowling in the fourth
Test at Headingley in 1972. Fungus had
attacked the wicket and Underwood was
at his deadliest.

138
Bob Massie bowling at Lord's in 1972
when he took eight English wickets in
each innings. His sixteen wickets is
second only to Laker's nineteen in England
—Australia matches.

139

139
The England team for the final Test match at the Oval in 1972. *Back row:* J. Hampshire, G. Arnold, A. Greig, D. Underwood, B. Wood, A. Knott. *Front row:* P. Parfitt, B. D'Oliveira, R. Illingworth (captain), J. Edrich, J. Snow.

140
A fine picture of John Edrich off-driving. Rod Marsh is behind the stumps.

141
The fifth Test at the Oval, 1972, and a near thing for Ian Chappell as a return from Tony Greig hits the wicket.

142
Paul Sheahan seeing Australia to victory at the Oval, 1972.

143
Part of Underwood's field for the fourth Test of 1972. Peter Parfitt catches Doug Walters.

140

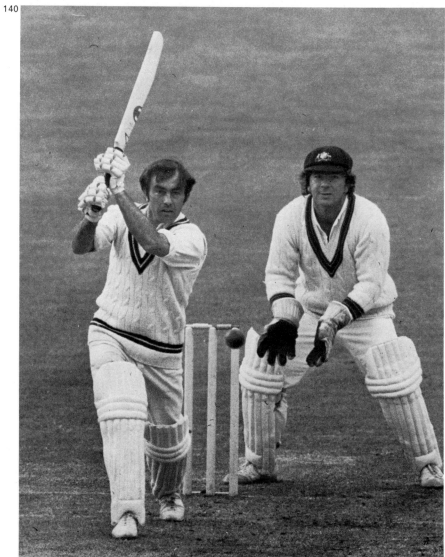

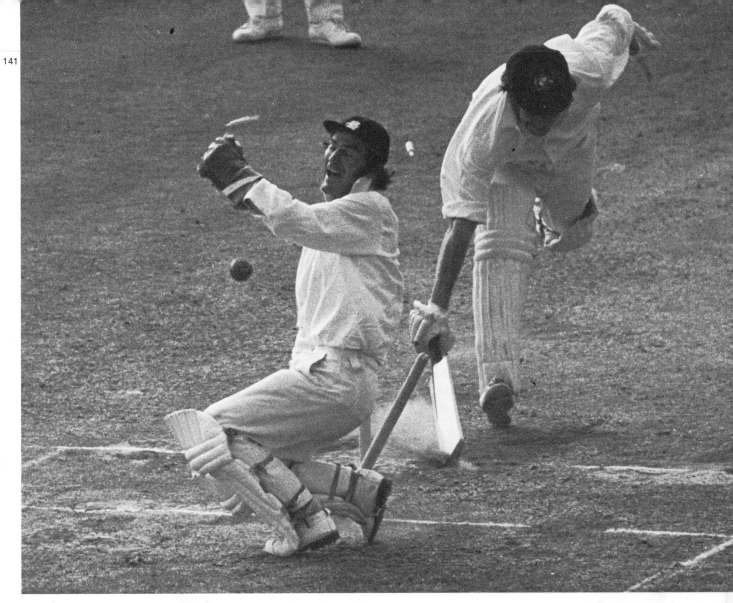

141

142

143

144

The second Test at Perth in the 1974–75 series and Doug Walters hooks, on his way to 103.

144

146

147

Thomson bowls a no-ball to Cowdrey in the third Test at Melbourne, 1974–75, and Rod Marsh makes a great leap to stop the ball.

148

One of Jeff Thomson's 33 wickets in the 1974–75 series. Tony Greig is caught by Greg Chappell in the slips.

149

Ross Edwards on his way to 115 in the second Test at Perth, 1974–75, drives Bob Willis through the covers for four.

145

145

Ian Redpath bisects the umpire and the non-striker with a straight drive.

146

Terry Jenner bowling in the 1974–75 series.

147

149 CRICKET AWARDS

1974-75
Australia 4
England 1

The 1974–75 series can be summed up in two words: Lillee and Thomson. Jeff Thomson, making his debut against England, joined Dennis Lillee, returning after a serious back injury, to form a match-winning partnership of fast bowlers to match Trueman and Statham and Lindwall and Miller.

In the first Test, after Australia scored 309, Thomson had both England openers out for 10, and despite a dashing 110 by Greig, Australia led by 44 runs. Six wickets for 46 by Thomson in the second innings gave Australia a win by 166. Cowdrey was flown out to bolster the England batting in the second Test, but Lillee and Thomson were too fast again and centuries by Ross Edwards and Walters helped Australia to a nine-wicket win.

Melbourne provided the closest match of the series: England 242 and 244, Australia 241 and 238 for 8, needing eight more runs with two wickets left. In this match Dennis Amiss launched a scintillating attack on Lillee and Thomson, only to fall to Ashley Mallett at 90.

At Sydney, Mike Denness, the England captain, dropped himself and Rick McCosker was brought in to the Australian side for his first Test and made 80, Australia getting a lead of 110. Second-innings centuries from Redpath and Greg Chappell enabled Australia to win by 171.

By this time behaviour on the field was causing many cricket lovers concern. Lillee had said that his bouncers were intended to hit the batsmen (and they were succeeding) and threats and swearing

were said to form part of the exchanges between opposing players.

Australia won the fifth Test easily, despite eleven wickets for Underwood and 106 not out from Knott. Thomson could not play in the sixth Test because of an injury acquired at tennis, and England won by an innings. Greg Chappell scored 102 and Max Walker took 8 wickets for 143, but fine bowling by Peter Lever (6 for 38 and 3 for 65) and successive stands of 149 between Edrich (70) and Denness (188), 192 between Denness and Fletcher (146) and 148 between Fletcher and Greig (89) were more than enough.

On this tour England badly missed Boycott, who declined the invitation, and Snow, who wasn't given one, but the series belonged emphatically to Lillee (25 wickets) and Thomson (33 wickets).

150

AUSTRALIA

151						
I. R. Redpath	b Willis	5	b Willis	25		
W. J. Edwards	c Amiss b Hendrick	4	c Knott b Willis	5		
I. M. Chappell	c Greig b Willis	90	c Fletcher b Underwood	11		
G. S. Chappell	c Fletcher b Underwood	58	b Underwood	71		
R. Edwards	c Knott b Underwood	32	c Knott b Willis	53		
K. D. Walters	c Lever b Willis	3	not out	62		
R. W. Marsh	c Denness b Hendrick	14	not out	46		
T. J. Jenner	c Lever b Willis	12				
D. K. Lillee	c Knott b Greig	15				
M. H. Walker	not out	41				
J. R. Thomson	run out	23				
Extras	(lb 4, nb 8)	12	(b 1, lb 7, w 1, nb 6)	15		
Total		**309**	**Total** (5 wkts dec)	**288**		

FALL OF WICKETS
AUSTRALIA

Wkt.	1st	2nd
1st	7	15
2nd	10	39
3rd	110	59
4th	197	173
5th	202	190
6th	205	—
7th	228	—
8th	229	—
9th	257	—
10th	309	—

ENGLAND

D. L. Amiss	c Jenner b Thomson	7	c Walters b Thomson	25
B. W. Luckhurst	c Marsh b Thomson	1	c Chappell I. b Lillee	3
J. H. Edrich	c Chappell I. b Thomson	48	b Thomson	6
M. H. Denness	lbw Walker	6	c Walters b Thomson	27
K. W. Fletcher	b Lillee	17	c Chappell G. b Jenner	19
A. W. Greig	c Marsh b Lillee	110	b Thomson	2
A. P. E. Knott	c Jenner b Walker	12	b Thomson	19
P. Lever	c Chappell I. b Walker	4	c Redpath b Lillee	14
D. L. Underwood	c Redpath b Walters	25	c Walker b Jenner	30
M. Hendrick	c Redpath b Walker	4	b Thomson	0
R. G. D. Willis	not out	13	not out	3
Extras	(b 5, lb 2, w 3, nb 8)	18	(b 8, lb 3, w 2, nb 5)	18
Total		**265**	**Total**	**166**

ENGLAND

Wkt.	1st	2nd
1st	9	18
2nd	10	40
3rd	33	44
4th	57	92
5th	130	94
6th	162	94
7th	168	115
8th	226	162
9th	248	163
10th	265	166

UMPIRES:
T. F. BROOKS,
R. C. BAILHACHE

ENGLAND

	1st Innings				2nd Innings			
	O	M	R	W	O	M	R	W
Willis	21·5	3	56	4	15	3	45	3
Lever	16	1	53	0	18	4	58	0
Hendrick	19	3	64	2	13	2	47	0
Greig	16	2	70	1	13	2	60	0
Underwood	20	6	54	2	26	6	63	2

AUSTRALIA

	1st Innings				2nd Innings			
	O	M	R	W	O	M	R	W
Lillee	23	6	73	2	12	2	25	2
Thomson	21	5	59	3	17·5	3	46	6
Walker	24·5	2	73	4	9	4	32	0
Walters	6	1	18	1	2	2	0	0
Jenner	6	1	24	0	16	5	45	2

153

154

150
Dennis Amiss batting in the third Test at Melbourne, 1974–75, when he scored a blistering 90.

151
The score-card for the first Test of the 1974–75 series at Brisbane, which gave the first warning to England of the menace of the Lillee–Thomson combination.

152
Bob Willis, who made two tours of Australia, 1970–71 and 1974–75, before he'd played against the Aussies at home.

153
Max Walker, great medium pace support for Lillee and Thomson, made his debut against England in the 1974–75 series.

154
Jeff Thomson, Australian fast bowling find of 1974, bowling at Headingley in 1975.

155
Dennis Lillee bowling in the second Test at Lord's in 1975.

155

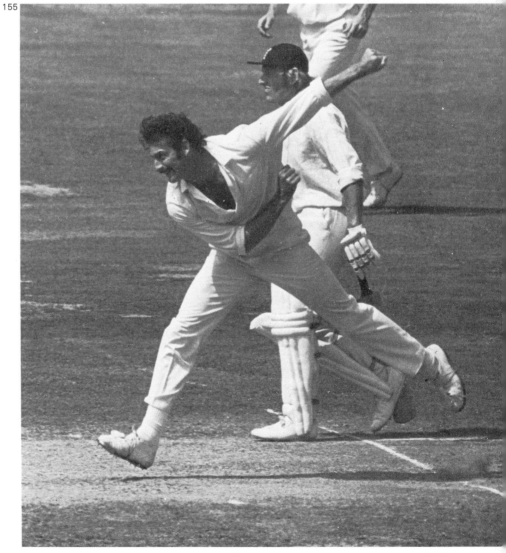

156

157

156
Fred Titmus, who came back to Test
bowling after losing toes in an accident
in the West Indies, bowling in the third
Test at Melbourne, 1974–75.

157
Australia's off-spinner of the 1970s,
Ashley Mallett, bowling against England
at the Oval, 1975.

158
Mike Denness captained the England team
to Australia in 1974–75, but lost the
captaincy to Tony Greig after the first
Test match of 1975.

159
Ross Edwards played thirteen times
against England and hit two centuries.
The wicket keeper is John Murray.

160
Keith Fletcher's first century against
Australia came in the final Test at
Melbourne, 1974–75, when he scored
146 and added 192 with Mike Denness
for the fourth wicket.

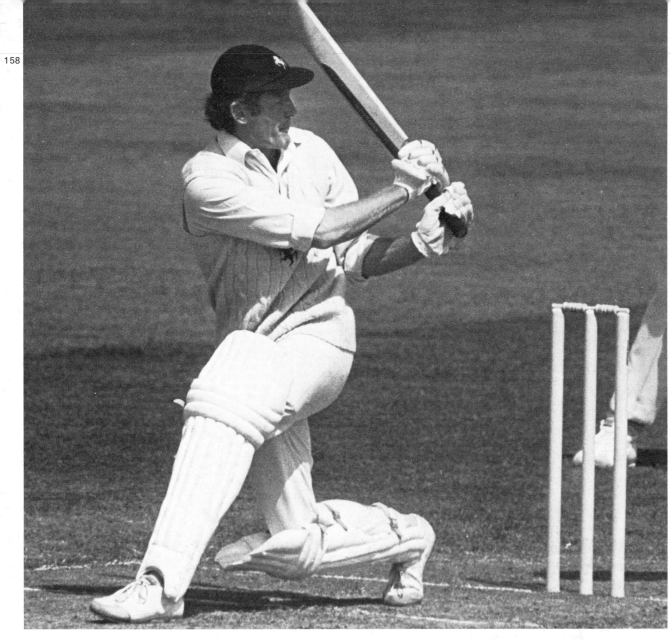

158

159

160

1975
England 0
Australia 1

A four-match series in 1975 was decided by the first Test. Denness put Australia in at Edgbaston on a grey day but Australia scored 359, and it was England who were caught by the rain, and put out for 101 and 173, Graham Gooch joining other distinguished batsmen in getting a pair in his first Test. This decision cost Denness his place, and Tony Greig took over as England captain. David Steele and Bob Woolmer made their Test debuts at Lord's, and grey-haired, bespectacled, 33-year-old Steele became a folk hero, doing well in each of his six innings in the series. England had the better of the match, a fine second innings 175 by Edrich allowing them to declare and set Australia 484 to win, but at 329

163

164

165

161
David Steele made his Test debut against Australia in 1975 and in six innings scored 50, 45, 73, 92, 39 and 66.

162
The Australians in 1975. *Back row:* A. Mallett, G. Gilmour, D. Lillee, J. Thomson, A. Hurst, M. Walker, R. McCosker, A. Turner. *Front row:* R. Edwards, D. Walters, I. Chappell (captain), G. Chappell, R. Marsh, B. Laird.

163
Ian Chappell, Australia's captain, batting in the third Test at Headingley, 1975. Knott is keeping wicket.

164
John Snow, England's best fast bowler of the late 1960s and early 1970s, bowling in the third Test at Headingley in 1975.

165
Chris Old, England's fast bowler and hard-hitting lower order batsman, made his debut against Australia on the 1974–75 tour.

for 3 Australia comfortably saved the game.

England pressed for a win again in the third Test, in which Phil Edmonds took 5 for 28 on his Test debut, giving England a lead of 153. Gary Gilmour, playing in his first Test against England, followed a first innings 6 for 85 with 3 for 72, and England, all out 291, set Australia 445 to win. At 220 for 3 (McCosker 95 not out) at the end of the fourth day, Australia were putting up a fight, but vandals got into the ground in the early hours of the morning and dug holes and poured oil on the pitch. The match was abandoned as a draw, and a potentially exciting match ruined.

England's chance of levelling the series diminished rapidly on the first day of the final Test as McCosker (127) and Ian Chappell (192) added 277 for the second wicket, Australia finally declaring at 532 for 9. England followed on, but a long innings of 149 by Bob Woolmer in a total of 538 ensured the draw.

166

166
Bob Woolmer made his first appearance against the Australians in 1975 and in his second Test saved the game with an innings of 149.

167
Gary Gilmour, in his first Test against England at Headingley in 1975, took 9 wickets for 157.

167

168
The third Test at Headingley in 1975 was ended when the pitch was ruined in the early hours of the morning of the fifth day by campaigners attempting to get an investigation into a prison sentence. The rival captains Tony Greig and Ian Chappell inspecting the damage.

169
Rick McCosker driving against Willis during his Test debut innings at Sydney in the 1974–75 series. He went on to make 80.

170
Phil Edmonds, who made his Test debut in the third Test at Headingley in 1975, bowled Ian Chappell in his second over, and had 5 for 17 after his first twelve overs in Test cricket.

170

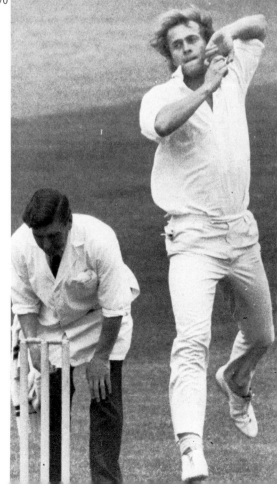

TEST APPEARANCES 1877–1976

The following is a complete list of those who have played in Test matches between England and Australia, together with the number of England–Australia Tests in which they have played and the seasons in which they made their first and last appearances in such Tests. For Australian seasons, the year in which the season began is given, i.e. 1974 indicates season 1974–75; 1876 indicates 1876–77.

ENGLAND

Abel, R. 11 (1888–1902)
Absolom, C. A. 1 (1878)
Allen, D. A. 10 (1961–65)
Allen, G. O. 13 (1930–36)
Ames, L. E. G. 17 (1932–38)
Amiss, D. L. 8 (1968–75)
Andrew, K. V. 1 (1954)
Appleyard, R. 5 (1954–56)
Armitage, T. 2 (1876)
Arnold, E. G. 8 (1903–05)
Arnold, G. G. 8 (1972–75)
Attewell, W. 6 (1884–91)

Bailey, T. E. 23 (1950–58)
Barber, R. W. 7 (1964–68)
Barlow, R. G. 17 (1881–86)
Barnes, S. F. 20 (1901–12)
Barnes, W. 21 (1880–86)
Barnett, C. J. 9 (1936–48)
Barrington, K. F. 23 (1961–68)
Bates, W. 15 (1881–86)
Bean, G. 3 (1891)
Bedser, A. V. 21 (1946–54)
Bligh, Hon. Ivo 4 (1882)
Blythe, C. 9 (1901–09)
Bosanquet, B. J. T. 7 (1903–05)
Bowes, W. E. 6 (1932–38)
Boycott, G. 19 (1964–72)
Bradley, W. M. 2 ((1889)
Braund, L. C. 20 (1901–07)
Brearley, W. 3 (1905–09)
Briggs, J. 31 (1886–99)
Brockwell, W. 7 (1893–99)
Brown, D. J. 8 (1965–68)
Brown, F. R. 6 (1950–53)
Brown, G. 3 (1921)
Brown, J. T. 8 (1894–99)

Carr, A. W. 4 (1926)
Carr, D. W. 1 (1909)
Cartwright, T. W. 2 (1964)
Chapman, A. P. F. 16 (1924–30)
Charlwood, H. 2 (1876)
Christopherson, S. 1 (1884)
Clark, E. W. 2 (1934)
Close, D. B. 2 (1950–61)
Coldwell, L. J. 4 (1962–64)
Compton, D. C. S. 28 (1938–56)
Cowdrey, M. C. 43 (1954–74)
Coxon, A. 1 (1948)
Cranston, J. 1 (1890)
Cranston, K. 1 (1948)
Crapp, J. F. 3 (1948)
Crawford, J. N. 5 (1907)

Dean, H. 2 (1912)
Denness, M. H. 6 (1974–75)
Denton, D. 1 (1905)
Dewes, J. G. 3 (1948–50)
Dexter, E. R. 19 (1958–68)
Dipper, A. E. 1 (1921)
d'Oliveira, B. L. 13 (1968–72)
Dollery, H. E. 2 (1948)
Dolphin, A. 1 (1920)
Douglas, J. W. H. T. 17 (1911–24)
Druce, N. F. 5 (1897)
Ducat, A. N. 1 (1921)
Duckworth, G. 10 (1928–30)
Duleepsinhji, K. S. 4 (1930)
Durston, F. J. 1 (1921)

Edmonds, P. H. 2 (1975)
Edrich, J. H. 32 (1964–75)
Edrich, W. J. 21 (1938–54)
Emmett, G. M. 1 (1948)
Emmett, T. 7 (1876–81)
Evans, A. J. 1 (1921)
Evans, T. G. 31 (1946–58)

Fagg, A. E. 2 (1936)
Fane, F. L. 4 (1907)
Farnes, K. 8 (1934–38)
Fender, P. G. H. 5 (1920–21)
Fielder, A. 6 (1903–07)
Fishlock, L. B. 1 (1946)

Flavell, J. A. 4 (1961–64)
Fletcher, K. W. R. 14 (1968–75)
Flowers, W. 8 (1884–93)
Ford, F. G. 5 (1894)
Foster, F. R. 8 (1911–12)
Foster, R. E. 5 (1903)
Freeman, A. P. 2 (1924)
Fry, C. B. 18 (1899–1912)

Gay, L. H. 1 (1894)
Geary, G. 9 (1926–34)
Gibb, P. A. 1 (1946)
Gifford, N. 5 (1964–72)
Gilligan, A. E. R. 5 (1924)
Goddard, T. W. 1 (1930)
Gooch, G. A. 2 (1975)
Grace, E. M. 1 (1880)
Grace, G. F. 1 (1880)
Grace, W. G. 22 (1880–99)
Graveney, T. W. 22 (1953–68)
Greenwood, A. 2 (1876)
Greig, A. W. 15 (1972–75)
Gunn, G. 11 (1907–11)
Gunn, J. 6 (1901–05)
Gunn, W. 11 (1886–99)

Haig, N. E. 1 (1921)
Haigh, S. 4 (1905–12)
Hallows, C. 1 (1921)
Hammond, W. R. 33 (1928–46)
Hampshire, J. H. 4 (1970–75)
Hardinge, H. T. W. 1 (1921)
Hardstaff, J. 5 (1907)
Hardstaff, J. Jnr. 9 (1936–48)
Harris, Lord 4 (1878–84)
Hayes, E. G. 1 (1909)
Hayward, T. W. 29 (1896–1909)
Hearne, J. T. 11 (1896–99)
Hearne, J. W. 16 (1911–26)
Hendren, E. H. 28 (1920–34)
Hendrick, M. 2 (1974)
Higgs, K. 2 (1965–68)
Hill, A. 2 (1876)
Hirst, G. H. 21 (1897–1909)
Hitch, J. W. 6 (1911–21)
Hobbs, J. B. 41 (1907–30)
Hollies, W. E. 1 (1948)
Holmes, P. 1 (1921)
Hone, L. 1 (1878)
Hopwood, J. L. 2 (1934)
Hornby, A. N. 3 (1878–84)
Howell, H. 4 (1920–21)
Humphries, J. 3 (1907)
Hunter, J. 5 (1884)
Hutchings, K. L. 7 (1902–07)
Hutton, L. 27 (1938–54)

Ikin, J. T. 5 (1946)
Illingworth, R. 18 (1961–72)
Insole, D. J. 1 (1956)

Jackson, F. S. 20 (1893–1905)
Jackson, H. L. 1 (1961)
Jardine, D. R. 10 (1928–32)
Jessop, G. L. 13 (1899–1909)
Jones, A. O. 12 (1899–1909)
Jones, I. J. 4 (1965)
Jupp, H. 2 (1876)
Jupp, V. W. C. 2 (1921)

Keeton, W. W. 1 (1934)
Kenyon, D. 2 (1953)
Kilner, R. 7 (1924–26)
King, J. H. 1 (1909)
Kinneir, S. P. 1 (1911)
Knight, A. E. 3 (1903)
Knight, B. R. 5 (1962–68)
Knight, D. J. 1 (1921)
Knott, A. P. E. 26 (1968–75)

Laker, J. C. 15 (1948–58)
Larwood, H. 15 (1926–32)
Leslie, C. F. H. 4 (1882)
Lever, P. 9 (1970–75)
Leyland, M. 20 (1928–38)
Lilley, A. A. 32 (1896–1909)
Lillywhite, Jas. Jnr. 2 (1876)
Lloyd, D. 4 (1974)

Loader, P. J. 2 (1958)
Lock, G. A. R. 13 (1953–61)
Lockwood, W. H. 12 (1893–1902)
Lohmann, G. A. 15 (1886–96)
Lucas, A. P. 5 (1878–84)
Luckhurst, B. W. 11 (1970–74)
Lyttelton, Hon. A. 4 (1880–84)

Macaulay, G. G. 1 (1926)
McGahey, C. P. 2 (1901)
MacGregor, G. 8 (1890–93)
McIntyre, A. J. W. 1 (1950)
MacKinnon, F. A. 1 (1878)
MacLaren, A. C. 35 (1894–1909)
Makepeace, H. 4 (1920)
Martin, F. 1 (1890)
Mason, J. R. 5 (1897)
May, P. B. H. 21 (1953–61)
Mead, C. P. 7 (1911–28)
Mead, W. 1 (1899)
Midwinter, W. E. 4 (1881)
Milburn, C. 2 (1968)
Milton, C. A. 2 (1958)
Mitchell, T. B. 3 (1932–34)
Mold, A. 3 (1893)
Morley, F. 4 (1880–82)
Mortimore, J. B. 2 (1958–64)
Moss, A. E. 1 (1956)
Murray, J. T. 6 (1961–62)

Newham, W. 1 (1887)
Nichols, M. S. 1 (1930)

Oakman, A. S. M. 2 (1956)
O'Brien, T. C. 2 (1884–88)
Old, C. M. 5 (1974–75)

Palairet, L. C. H. 2 (1902)
Parfitt, P. H. 9 (1962–72)
Parker, C. W. L. 1 (1921)
Parkhouse, W. G. A. 2 (1950)
Parkin, C. H. 9 (1920–21)
Parks, J. M. 10 (1964–65)
Pataudi, Nawab of 3 (1932–34)
Paynter, E. 7 (1932–38)
Peate, E. 9 (1881–86)
Peebles, I. A. R. 2 (1930)
Peel, R. 20 (1884–96)
Penn, F. 1 (1880)
Philipson, H. 5 (1891–94)
Pilling, R. 8 (1881–88)
Pocock, P. I. 1 (1968)
Pollard, R. 2 (1948)
Price, J. S. E. 3 (1964–72)
Price, W. F. 1 (1938)
Prideaux, R. M. 1 (1968)
Pullar, G. 9 (1961–62)

Quaife, W. G. 7 (1899–1901)

Ranjitsinhji, K. S. 15 (1896–1902)
Read, J. M. 15 (1882–93)
Read, W. W. 17 (1882–93)
Relf, A. E. 3 (1903–09)
Rhodes, W. 41 (1899–1926)
Richardson, P. E. 9 (1956–58)
Richardson, T. 14 (1893–97)
Richmond, T. L. 1 (1921)
Robins, R. W. V. 6 (1930–36)
Roope, G. R. J. 1 (1975)
Root, C. F. 3 (1926)
Royle, V. P. F. A. 1
Rumsey, F. E. 1 (1964)
Russell, A. C. 6 (1920–21)
Russell, W. E. 1 (1965)

Sandham, A. 3 (1921–24)
Schultz, S. S. 1 (1878)
Scotton, W. H. 15 (1881–86)
Selby, J. 6 (1876–81)
Sharp, J. 3 (1909)
Sharpe, J. W. 3 (1890–91)
Sharpe, P. J. 2 (1964)
Shaw, A. 7 (1876–81)
Sheppard, Rt. Rev. D. S. 9 (1950–62)
Sherwin, M. 3 (1886–88)

Shrewsbury, A. 23 (1881–93)
Shuter, J. 1 (1888)
Shuttleworth, K. 2 (1970)
Simpson, R. T. 9 (1950–54)
Sims, J. M. 2 (1936)
Sinfield, R. A. 1 (1938)
Smith, A. C. 4 (1962)
Smith, E. J. 7 (1911–12)
Smith, M. J. K. 9 (1961–72)
Smith, T. P. B. 2 (1946)
Snow, J. A. 20 (1968–75)
Southerton, J. 2 (1876)
Spooner, R. H. 7 (1905–12)
Statham, J. B. 22 (1953–62)
Steel, A. G. 13 (1880–88)
Steele, D. S. 3 (1975)
Stevens, G. T. S. 2 (1926)
Stoddart, A. E. 16 (1887–97)
Storer, W. 6 (1897–99)
Strudwick, H. 17 (1911–26)
Studd, C. T. 5 (1882)
Studd, G. B. 4 (1882)
Subba Row, R. 5 (1961)
Sugg, F. H. 2 (1888)
Sutcliffe, H. 27 (1924–34)
Swetman, R. 2 (1958)

Tate, F. W. 1 (1902)
Tate, M. W. 20 (1924–30)
Tattersall, R. 3 (1950–53)
Taylor, K. 1 (1964)
Tennyson, Hon. L. H. 4 (1921)
Thompson, G. J. 1 (1909)
Titmus, F. J. 19 (1962–74)
Townsend, C. L. 1 (1899)
Trueman, F. S. 19 (1953–62)
Tyldesley, E. 5 (1921–28)
Tyldesley, J. T. 26 (1899–1909)
Tyldesley, R. 3 (1924–30)
Tylecote, E. F. S. 6 (1882–86)
Tyson, F. H. 8 (1954–58)

Ulyett, G. 23 (1876–90)

Underwood, D. L. 20 (1968–74)

Verity, H. 18 (1932–38)
Vernon, G. F. 1 (1882)
Vine, J. 2 (1911)
Voce, W. 11 (1932–46)

Waddington, A. 2 (1920)
Wainwright, E. 5 (1893–97)
Walters, C. F. 5 (1934)
Ward, A. 7 (1893–94)
Wardle, J. H. 8 (1953–56)
Warner, P. F. 7 (1903–12)
Warr, J. J. 2 (1950)
Warren, A. R. 1 (1905)
Washbrook, C. 17 (1946–56)
Watkins, A. J. 1 (1948)
Watson, W. 7 (1953–58)
Webbe, A. J. 1 (1878)
Wellard, A. W. 1 (1938)
White, J. C. 7 (1921–30)
Whysall, W. W. 4 (1924–30)
Willis, R. G. D. 9 (1970–74)
Wilson, E. R. 1 (1920)
Wood, A. 1 (1938)
Wood, B. 4 (1972–75)
Wood, H. 1 (1888)
Wood, R. 1 (1886)
Woolley, F. E. 32 (1909–34)
Woolmer, R. A. 2 (1975)
Worthington, T. S. 3 (1936)
Wright, D. V. P. 14 (1938–50)
Wyatt, R. E. S. 12 (1930–36)
Wynyard, E. G. 1 (1896)

Yardley, N. W. D. 10 (1946–48)
Young, H. 2 (1899)
Young, J. A. 3 (1948)
Young, R. A. 2 (1907)

AUSTRALIA

A'Beckett, E. L. 3 (1928–30)
Alexander, G. 2 (1880–84)
Alexander, H. H. 1 (1932)
Allan, F. E. 1 (1878)
Allan, P. J. 1 (1965)
Allen, R. C. 1 (1886)
Andrews, T. J. E. 13 (1921–26)
Archer, K. A. 3 (1950)
Archer, R. G. 12 (1953–56)
Armstrong, W. W. 42 (1901–21)

Badcock, C. L. 7 (1936–38)
Bannerman, A. C. 28 (1878–93)
Bannerman, C. 3 (1876–78)
Bardsley, W. 30 (1909–26)
Barnes, S. G. 9 (1938–48)
Barnett, B. A. 4 (1938)
Barrett, J. E. 2 (1890)
Benaud, R. 27 (1953–62)
Blackham, J. M. 35 (1876–94)
Blackie, D. J. 3 (1928)
Bonnor, G. J. 17 (1880–88)
Booth, B. C. 15 (1961–65)
Boyle, H. F. 12 (1878–84)
Bradman, D. G. 37 (1928–48)
Bromley, E. H. 2 (1932–34)
Brown, W. A. 13 (1934–48)
Bruce, W. 14 (1884–94)
Burge, P. J. 22 (1954–65)
Burke, J. W. 14 (1950–58)
Burn, K. E. 2 (1890)
Burton, F. J. 2 (1886–87)

Callaway, S. T. 3 (1891–94)
Carkeek, W. 3 (1912)
Carter, H. 21 (1907–21)
Chappell, G. S. 20 (1970–75)
Chappell, I. M. 28 (1965–75)
Charlton, P. C. 2 (1890)
Chipperfield, A. G. 9 (1936–38)
Colley, D. J. 3 (1972)
Collins, H. L. 16 (1920–26)
Coningham, A. 1 (1894)
Connolly, A. N. 7 (1965–70)
Cooper, B. B. 1 (1876)
Cooper, W. H. 2 (1881–84)
Corling, G. E. 5 (1964)
Cottam, W. J. 1 (1886)
Cotter, A. B. 16 (1903–11)
Coultard, G. 1 (1881)
Cowper, R. M. 9 (1964–68)
Craig, I. D. 2 (1956)
Crawford, P. 1 (1956)

Darling, J. 31 (1894–1905)
Darling, L. S. 7 (1932–36)
Davidson, A. K. 25 (1953–62)
De Courcy, J. H. 3 (1953)
Dell, A. R. 1 (1970)
Donnan, H. 5 (1891–96)
Dooland, B. 2 (1946)
Duff, R. A. 19 (1901–05)
Duncan, J. R. F. 1 (1970)
Dymock, G. 1 (1974)

Eady, C. J. 2 (1896–1901)
Eastwood, K. H. 1 (1970)
Ebling, H. I. 1 (1934)
Edwards, J. D. 3 (1888)
Edwards, R. 13 (1972–75)
Edwards, W. J. 3 (1974)
Emery, S. H. 2 (1912)
Evans, E. 6 (1881–86)

Fairfax, A. G. 5 (1928–30)
Favell, L. E. 6 (1954–58)
Ferris, J. J. 8 (1886–90)
Fingleton, J. H. 12 (1932–38)
Fleetwood-Smith, L. O'B.
  7 (1936–38)
Francis, B. C. 3 (1972)
Freeman, E. W. 2 (1968)
Freer, F. W. 1 (1946)

Garrett, T. W. 19 (1876–87)
Gaunt, R. A. 1 (1961)
Gehrs, D. R. A. 4 (1903–05)
Giffen, G. 31 (1881–96)
Giffen, W. F. 3 (1886–91)
Gilmour, G. J. 1 (1975)
Gleeson, J. W. 13 (1968–72)
Graham, H. 6 (1893–96)
Gregory, D. W. 3 (1876–78)
Gregory, E. J. 1 (1876)
Gregory, J. M. 21 (1920–28)
Gregory, R. G. 2 (1936)
Gregory, S. E. 52 (1890–1912)
Grimmett, C. V. 22 (1924–34)

Groube, T. U. 1 (1880)
Grout, A. T. W. 22 (1958–65)
Guest, C. E. J. 1 (1962)

Hamence, R. A. 1 (1946)
Harry, J. 1 (1894)
Hartigan, R. J. 2 (1907)
Hartkopf, A. E. V. 1 (1924)
Harvey, M. R. 1 (1946)
Harvey, R. N. 37 (1948–62)
Hassett, A. L. 24 (1938–53)
Hawke, N. J. N. 12 (1962–68)
Hazlitt, G. R. 6 (1907–12)
Hendry, H. L. 9 (1921–28)
Hill, C. 41 (1896–1911)
Hill, J. C. 2 (1953)
Hodges, J. 1 (1876)
Hole, G. B. 9 (1950–54)
Hopkins, A. J. 17 (1901–09)
Horan, T. P. 15 (1876–84)
Hordern, H. V. 5 (1911)
Hornibrook, P. M. 6 (1928–30)
Howell, W. P. 16 (1897–1903)

Inverarity, R. J. 5 (1968–72)
Iredale, F. A. 14 (1894–99)
Ironmonger, H. 6 (1928–32)
Iverson, J. B. 5 (1950)

Jackson, A. A. 4 (1928–30)
Jarman, B. N. 7 (1962–68)
Jarvis, A. H. 11 (1884–94)
Jenner, T. J. 4 (1970–74)
Jennings, C. B. 3 (1912)
Johnson, I. W. 22 (1946–56)
Johnston, W. A. 17 (1948–54)
Jones, E. 18 (1894–1902)
Jones, S. P. 12 (1881–87)

Kelleway, C. 18 (1911–28)
Kelly, J. J. 33 (1896–1905)
Kelly, T. J. D. 3 (1876–78)
Kendall, T. 2 (1876)
Kippax, A. F. 13 (1924–34)
Kline, L. F. 2 (1958)

Laver, F. 15 (1899–1909)
Langley, G. R. A. 9 (1953–56)
Lawry, W. M. 29 (1961–70)
Lee, P. K. 1 (1932)
Lillee, D. K. 17 (1970–75)
Lindwall, R. R. 29 (1946–58)
Love, H. S. 1 (1932)
Loxton, S. J. E. 6 (1948–50)
Lyons, J. J. 14 (1886–97)

McAlister, P. A. 8 (1903–09)
McCabe, S. J. 24 (1930–38)
Macartney, C. G. 26 (1907–26)
Mackay, K. D. 16 (1956–62)
McCool, C. L. 5 (1946)
McCormick, E. L. 7 (1936–38)
McCosker, R. B. 7 (1974–75)
McDonald, C. C. 15 (1954–61)
McDonald, E. A. 8 (1920–21)
McDonnell, P. S. 19 (1880–88)
McIlwraith, J. 1 (1886)
McKenzie, G. D. 25 (1961–70)
McKibbin, T. R. 5 (1894–97)
McLaren, J. W. 1 (1911)
McLeod, C. E. 17 (1894–1905)
McLeod, R. W. 6 (1893–96)
McShane, P. G. 3 (1884–87)
Maddocks, L. 5 (1954–56)
Mallett, A. A. 14 (1968–75)
Mailey, A. A. 18 (1920–26)
Marr, A. P. 1 (1884)
Marsh, R. W. 21 (1970–75)
Massie, H. H. 9 (1881–84)
Massie, R. A. L. 4 (1972)
Matthews, T. J. 5 (1911–12)
Mayne, E. R. 1 (1912)
Meckiff, I. 4 (1958)
Midwinter, W. E. 8 (1876–86)
Miller, K. R. 29 (1946–56)
Minnett, R. B. 6 (1911–12)
Misson, F. M. 2 (1961)
Moroney, J. R. 1 (1950)
Morris, A. R. 24 (1946–54)
Morris, S. 1 (1884)
Moses, H. 6 (1886–94)
Moule, W. H. 1 (1880)
Murdoch, W. L. 18 (1876–90)
Musgrove, H. 1 (1884)

Nagel, L. E. 1 (1932)
Nash, L. J. 1 (1936)
Noble, M. A. 39 (1897–1909)
Nothling, O. E. 1 (1928)

O'Brien, L. P. J. 3 (1932–36)
O'Connor, J. A. 4 (1907–09)
O'Keeffe, K. J. 2 (1970)
Oldfield, W. A. S. 38 (1920–36)
O'Neill, N. C. 19 (1958–64)
O'Reilly, W. J. 19 (1932–38)
Oxenham, R. K. 3 (1928)

Palmer, G. E. 17 (1880–86)
Park, R. L. 1 (1920)
Pellew, C. E. 9 (1920–21)
Philpott, P. I. 3 (1965)
Ponsford, W. H. 20 (1924–34)
Pope, R. J. 1 (1884)

Ransford, V. S. 15 (1907–11)
Redpath, I. R. 23 (1964–74)
Reedman, J. C. 1 (1894)
Richardson, A. J. 9 (1924–26)
Richardson, V. Y. 14 (1924–32)
Rigg, K. F. 3 (1936)
Ring, D. T. 2 (1948–53)
Robertson, W. R. 1 (1884)
Robinson, R. H. 1 (1936)
Rorke, G. F. 2 (1958)
Ryder, J. 17 (1920–28)

Saggers, R. A. 1 (1948)
Saunders, J. V. 12 (1901–07)
Scott, H. J. H. 8 (1884–86)
Sheahan, A. P. 9 (1968–72)
Shepherd, B. K. 2 (1962)
Sievers, M. W. S. 3 (1936)
Simpson, R. B. 19 (1958–65)
Sincock, D. J. 1 (1965)
Slater, K. N. 1 (1958)
Slight, J. 1 (1880)
Smith, D. 2 (1912)
Spofforth, F. R. 18 (1876–86)
Stackpole, K. R. 13 (1965–72)

Taber, H. B. 1 (1968)
Tallon, D. 15 (1946–53)
Taylor, J. M. 18 (1920–26)
Thomas, G. 3 (1965)
Thompson, N. 2 (1876)
Thomson, A. L. 4 (1970)
Thomson, J. R. 9 (1974–75)
Toshack, E. R. H. 9 (1946–48)
Travers, J. F. 1 (1901)
Tribe, G. E. 3 (1946)
Trott, A. E. 3 (1894)
Trott, G. H. S. 24 (1888–97)
Trumble, H. 30 (1890–1903)
Trumble, J. W. 7 (1884–86)
Trumper, V. T. 40 (1899–1911)
Turner, A. 3 (1975)
Turner, C. T. B. 17 (1886–1894)

Veivers, T. R. 9 (1964–65)

Waite, M. G. 2 (1938)
Walker, M. H. N. 10 (1974–75)
Wall, T. W. 14 (1928–34)
Walters, F. H. 1 (1884)
Walters, K. D. 30 (1965–75)
Ward, F. A. 4 (1936–38)
Watson, G. D. 2 (1972)
Watson, W. 1 (1954)
Whitty, W. J. 6 (1909–12)
Woodfull, W. M. 25 (1926–34)
Woods, S. M. J. 3 (1888)
Worrall, J. 11 (1884–99)

172
Australian captain in the centenary year,
Greg Chappell.

173
Cricket selectors. Australian Test selectors Dudley Seddon (*left*), Jack Ryder and Sir Donald Bradman.

174
Cricket captains. Ian Chappell and Mike Denness after the final Test of the 1974–75 series share a bottle of champagne.

175
Cricket dignitaries. English cricket chiefs wait for a taxi. *From left:* G. O. Allen, S. C. Griffith, F. R. Brown.

176
Wicket keepers. The rival wicket keepers of the 1970s. Alan Knott (England) batting, and Rod Marsh (Australia) keeping.

177
The England party leaving for India on their way to the Centenary Test in Melbourne. The players are (*front row from left*): Amiss, Willis, Lever (J. K.), Knott, Greig. On the gangplank from the top: Barlow, Underwood, Brearley, Selvey, Miller, Old (with Tolchard behind), Woolmer, Cope, Fletcher, Randall. Manager Barrington is next to Greig.

England v Australia
The Ashes

Season	England (Captains)	Australia (Captains)	Tests	Won by Eng.	Won by Aust.	Drawn
1876–77	James Lillywhite	D. W. Gregory	2	1	1	0
1878–79	Lord Harris	D. W. Gregory	1	0	1	0
1880	Lord Harris	W. L. Murdoch	1	1	0	0
1881–82	A. Shaw	W. L. Murdoch	4	0	2	2
1882	A. N. Hornby	W. L. Murdoch	1	0	1	0
1882–83	Hon. Ivo Bligh	W. L. Murdoch	4	2	2	0
1884	Lord Harris	W. L. Murdoch	3	1	0	2
1884–85	A. Shrewsbury	T. Horan	5	3	2	0
1886	A. G. Steel	H. J. H. Scott	3	3	0	0
1886–87	A. Shrewsbury	P. S. McDonnell	2	2	0	0
1887–88	W. W. Read	P. S. McDonnell	1	1	0	0
1888	W. G. Grace	P. S. McDonnell	3	2	1	0
1890	W. G. Grace	W. L. Murdoch	2	2	0	0
1891–92	W. G. Grace	J. M. Blackham	3	1	2	0
1893	W. G. Grace	J. M. Blackham	3	1	0	2
1894–95	A. E. Stoddart	G. Giffen	5	3	2	0
1896	W. G. Grace	G. H. S. Trott	3	2	1	0
1897–98	A. E. Stoddart	G. H. S. Trott	5	1	4	0
1899	A. C. MacLaren	J. Darling	5	0	1	4
1901–02	A. C. MacLaren	J. Darling	5	1	4	0
1902	A. C. MacLaren	J. Darling	5	1	2	2
1903–04	P. F. Warner	M. A. Noble	5	3	2	0
1905	Hon. F. S. Jackson	J. Darling	5	2	0	3
1907–08	A. O. Jones	M. A. Noble	5	1	4	0
1909	A. C. MacLaren	M. A. Noble	5	1	2	2
1911–12	J. W. H. T. Douglas	C. Hill	5	4	1	0
1912	C. B. Fry	S. E. Gregory	3	1	0	2
1920–21	J. W. H. T. Douglas	W. W. Armstrong	5	0	5	0
1921	Hon. L. H. Tennyson	W. W. Armstrong	5	0	3	2
1924–25	A. E. R. Gilligan	H. L. Collins	5	1	4	0
1926	A. W. Carr	H. L. Collins	5	1	0	4
1928–29	A. P. F. Chapman	J. Ryder	5	4	1	0
1930	A. P. F. Chapman	W. M. Woodfull	5	1	2	2
1932–33	D. R. Jardine	W. M. Woodfull	5	4	1	0
1934	R. E. S. Wyatt	W. M. Woodfull	5	1	2	2
1936–37	G. O. Allen	D. G. Bradman	5	2	3	0
1938	W. R. Hammond	D. G. Bradman	4	1	1	2
1946–47	W. R. Hammond	D. G. Bradman	5	0	3	2
1948	N. W. D. Yardley	D. G. Bradman	5	0	4	1
1950–51	F. R. Brown	A. L. Hassett	5	1	4	0
1953	L. Hutton	A. L. Hassett	5	1	0	4
1954–55	L. Hutton	I. W. Johnson	5	3	1	1
1956	P. B. H. May	I. W. Johnson	5	2	1	2
1958–59	P. B. H. May	R. Benaud	5	0	4	1
1961	P. B. H. May	R. Benaud	5	1	2	2
1962–63	E. R. Dexter	R. Benaud	5	1	1	3
1964	E. R. Dexter	R. B. Simpson	5	0	1	4
1965–66	M. J. K. Smith	R. B. Simpson	5	1	1	3
1968	M. C. Cowdrey	W. M. Lawry	5	1	1	3
1970–71	R. Illingworth	W. M. Lawry	6	2	0	4
1972	R. Illingworth	I. M. Chappell	5	2	2	1
1974–75	M. H. Denness	I. M. Chappell	6	1	4	1
1975	A. W. Greig	I. M. Chappell	4	0	1	3
In Australia			119	43	59	17
In England			105	28	28	49
Totals			224	71	87	66

Highest Totals for an Innings

By England			By Australia		
903 (7 wkts)	The Oval ..	1938	729 (6 wkts)	Lord's	1930
658 (8 wkts)	Nottingham.	1938	701	.. The Oval ...	1934
636	.. Sydney 1928–29		695	.. The Oval ..	1930
627 (9 wkts)	Manchester.	1934	659 (8 wkts)	Sydney 1946–47	
611	.. Manchester.	1964	656 (8 wkts)	Manchester.	1964
			645	.. Brisbane ...1946–47	
			604	.. Melbourne .1936–37	
			601 (8 wkts)	Brisbane ...1954–55	

Smallest Totals for an Innings

36 ..	Australia ..	Birmingham 1902	44 ..	Australia ..	The Oval 1896
42 ..	Australia ..	Sydney 1887–88	45 ..	England ..	Sydney 1886–87

Most Runs in a Rubber

England in England	 562	(av 62.44)	D. C. S. Compton ..	1948
England in Australia	 905	(av 113.12)	W. R. Hammond	1928–29
Australia in England	 974	(av 139.14)	D. G. Bradman	1930
Australia in Australia	 810	(av 90.00)	D. G. Bradman	1936–37

Most Wickets in a Rubber

England in England	 46	(av 9.60)	J. C. Laker	1956
England in Australia	 38	(av 23.18)	M. W. Tate	1924–25
Australia in England	 31	(av 17.67)	D. K. Lillee	1972
Australia in Australia	 36	(av 26.27)	A. A. Mailey	1920–21

Most Wickets in a Match

19 for 90	J. C. Laker for England	Manchester	1956
16 for 137	R. A. L. Massie for Australia	Lord's	1972
15 for 104	H. Verity for England	Lord's	1934
15 for 124	W. Rhodes for England	Melbourne	1903–04
14 for 90	F. R. Spofforth for Australia	The Oval	1882
14 for 99	A. V. Bedser for England	Nottingham	1953
14 for 102	W. Bates for England	Melbourne	1882–83

The Hat-Tricks

For England		For Australia	
W. Bates ..	Melbourne 1882–83	F. R. Spofforth	Melbourne 1878–79
J. Briggs ..	Sydney .. 1891–92	H. Trumble ..	Melbourne 1901–02
J. T. Hearne	Leeds .. 1899	H. Trumble ..	Melbourne 1903–04

Wicket-Keeping – Most Dismissals

	Matches	Caught	Stumped	Total
W. A. Oldfield (A.)	38	59	31	90
A. A. Lilley (E.)	32	65	19	84
A. P. E. Knott (E.)	26	75	8	83
A. T. W. Grout (A.)	22	69	7	76
T. G. Evans (E.)	31	63	12	75
R. W. Marsh (A.)	21	64	7	71

Scorers of Over 2,000 Runs

	Innings	Not Out	Runs	Highest Score	Average
D. G. Bradman ..	63	7	5,028	334	89·78
J. B. Hobbs	71	4	3,636	187	54·26
W. R. Hammond.	58	3	2,852	251	51·85
H. Sutcliffe	46	5	2,741	194	66·85
C. Hill	76	1	2,660	188	35·46
J. H. Edrich	57	3	2,644	175	48·96
M. C. Cowdrey ..	75	4	2,433	113	34·27
L. Hutton	49	6	2,428	364	56·46
R. N. Harvey....	68	5	2,416	167	38·34
V. T. Trumper ...	74	5	2,263	185	32·79
W. M. Lawry	51	5	2,233	166	48·54
S. E. Gregory ...	92	7	2,193	201	25·80
W. W. Armstrong.	71	9	2,172	158	35·03
K. F. Barrington .	39	6	2,111	256	63·96
A. R. Morris	43	2	2,080	206	50·73

Bowlers with 100 Wickets

	Balls	Runs	Wickets	5 Wkts. in Inns.	Average
H. Trumble ...	7,895	2,945	141	9	20·88
M. A. Noble ..	6,845	2,860	115	9	24·86
R. R. Lindwall .	6,728	2,559	114	6	22·44
W. Rhodes ...	5,791	2,616	109	6	24·00
S. F. Barnes ..	5,749	2,288	106	12	21·58
C. V. Grimmett .	9,224	3,439	106	11	32·44
A. V. Bedser ..	7,065	2,859	104	7	27·49
G. Giffen	6,325	2,791	103	7	27·09
W. J. O'Reilly .	7,864	2,587	102	8	25·36
R. Peel	5,216	1,715	102	6	16·81
C. T. B. Turner .	5,195	1,670	101	11	16·53

Record Partnerships for each Wicket

By England

323 for 1st	J. B. Hobbs and W. Rhodes at Melbourne	1911–12
382 for 2nd	L. Hutton and M. Leyland at The Oval	1938
262 for 3rd	W. R. Hammond and D. R. Jardine at Adelaide	1928–29
222 for 4th	W. R. Hammond and E. Paynter at Lord's	1938
206 for 5th	E. Paynter and D. C. S. Compton at Nottingham	1938
215 for 6th	L. Hutton and J. Hardstaff at The Oval	1938
143 for 7th	F. E. Woolley and J. Vine at Sydney	1911–12
124 for 8th	E. H. Hendren and H. Larwood at Brisbane	1928–29
151 for 9th	W. H. Scotton and W. W. Read at The Oval	1884
130 for 10th	R. E. Foster and W. Rhodes at Sydney	1903–04

By Australia

244 for 1st	R. B. Simpson and W. M. Lawry at Adelaide	1965–66
451 for 2nd	W. H. Ponsford and D. G. Bradman at The Oval	1934
276 for 3rd	D. G. Bradman and A. L. Hassett at Brisbane	1946–47
388 for 4th	W. H. Ponsford and D. G. Bradman at Leeds	1934
405 for 5th	S. G. Barnes and D. G. Bradman at Sydney	1946–47
346 for 6th	J. H. Fingleton and D. G. Bradman at Melbourne	1936–37
165 for 7th	C. Hill and H. Trumble at Melbourne	1897–98
243 for 8th	R. J. Hartigan and C. Hill at Adelaide	1907–08
154 for 9th	S. E. Gregory and J. M. Blackham at Sydney	1894–95
127 for 10th	J. M. Taylor and A. A. Mailey at Sydney	1924–25

178
The Kennington Oval Cricket Ground.

Acknowledgements

The photographs in this book came from the following sources:

Australian News and Information Bureau
Numbers 1, 36, 99, 110, 112, 114, 121, 123, 127, 128, 130, 147, 148, 149, 179.

Central Press Photos, London
Pictures facing title-page and on the foreword page. Numbers 35, 37, 38, 39, 40, 41, 43, 44, 45, 48, 49, 50, 51, 52, 53, 54, 55, 57, 58, 59, 60, 61, 62, 64, 65–69, 71, 72, 73, 74, 75, 76, 77, 78, 79, 80, 81, 82, 83, 84, 85, 87, 89, 90, 91, 92, 93, 94, 96, 97, 98, 101, 102, 103, 106, 107, 108, 111, 113, 115, 117, 125, 139, 140, 159, 170, 173, 174, 175, 178.

The Mansell Collection
Front end paper. Numbers 2, 3, 4, 6, 7, 8, 9, 10, 11, 12, 13, 14, 15, 16, 17, 18, 19, 20, 22, 23, 24, 25, 26, 27, 28, 29, 30, 31, 32, 33, 34, 46, 47, 56, 69, 70, 88.

Patrick Eagar
Half-title picture. Back end-paper. Numbers 100, 104, 105, 109, 116, 118, 119, 120, 122, 124, 126, 129, 131, 132, 133, 134, 135, 136, 137, 138, 141, 142, 143, 144, 145, 146, 150, 152, 153, 154, 155, 156, 157, 158, 160, 161, 162, 163, 164, 165, 166, 167, 168, 169, 171, 172, 176. Colour pictures on cover.

Syndication International, London
177.

179
The Melbourne Cricket Club museum contains many rare momentoes including these cricket balls and baseballs. The oldest ball, bottom left, dates from 1860, seventeen years before the first Test.